W9-BWN-273

Come on a journey across the desert sands of North Africa, toward a wonderful and mysterious place called Giza. Throughout history, people have gone to Giza hoping to find hidden treasures. It is still a place of many unsolved mysteries.

This is a journey through time as well as space. We are traveling back 4,500 years to one of the earliest civilizations on Earth. Our destination is the land of ancient Egypt, ruled by pharaohs— kings who were thought to become gods when they died.

JUN 2010

It took more than 20 years to build the Great Pyramid of Giza. Many thousands of Egyptians worked on its construction, on behalf of their king, the great pharaoh Khufu. This is the story of how, and why, the pyramid was built.

As Giza comes into view, there is an amazing sight in front of us— a group of vast stone buildings with triangular sides and square bases. These are pyramids. The biggest and oldest at Giza is called the Great Pyramid.

PYRAMID

written by
PETER CHRISP

EARLY DESCRIPTIONS

THE PYRAMIDS IN HISTORY

For more than 4,500 years, three great pyramids have stood in the desert sand at Giza in Egypt. They were built by ancient Egyptian kings called pharaohs—rulers of the first united nation-state in history.

Riddle in the sand

The pharaohs who erected these massive stone monuments left no writings explaining how or why they had gone about making them. Generations of later visitors to Egypt have had to come up with their own explanations. Modern archaeologists (people who study the past by looking at ancient buildings, burials, and artifacts) have solved some of the mysteries surrounding the pyramids, but many others remain.

Early accounts

The oldest description of the pyramids was written by a Greek traveler, Herodotus (his portrait is shown above). He visited Egypt in the middle of the 5th century BC, when the pyramids were already over 2,000 years old. He questioned Egyptian priests, who explained that the pyramids were royal tombs. They also told him pyramid stories that had grown up over time. For example, the vast size of the greatest pyramid gave people the idea that it was built by a cruel tyrant who enslaved his population. The pharaoh's name was Khufu (known as Cheops in Greek). Herodotus wrote, "Cheops plunged into all manner of wickedness."

Tourist attraction

By the 2nd century BC, the pyramids were famous. The Greeks believed that they were the greatest of their Seven Wonders of the World.

Many people still think that slaves built the pyramids, as shown in this painting from the 1920s. This idea has now been proved wrong.

> "Mountains have been built on mountains. The size of the masonry is difficult for the mind to grasp."
>
> *Philo of Byzantium,* On the Seven Wonders, *c. 200 BC*

Writing in about 200 BC, a Greek called Philo of Byzantium declared: "Everyone is mystified at the enormous strength required to put up such a weight [of stone]… the whole polished work has been joined together so seamlessly that it seems to be made out of one continuous rock."

Roman visitors

After the Romans conquered Egypt in 30 BC, many Roman tourists went to see the pyramids for themselves. They were amazed at the skill shown in pyramid-building, yet they could not see the purrpose of the structures. In around AD 70, the Roman historian Pliny the Elder spluttered, "The pyramids… are a pointless and absurd display of royal wealth… these men showed much arrogance in the enterprise."

As if by magic

The Romans were followed by Arabs, who conquered Egypt in AD 642. The Arabs also found the pyramids baffling, and imagined that they must have been built using magic spells. In around AD 940, Arab writer Masoudi explained how this was done: "In carrying on the work, leaves of papyrus, or paper, inscribed with certain characters, were placed under the stones prepared in the quarries. Upon being struck, the blocks were moved at each time the distance of an arrow shot, and so by degrees [they] arrived at the pyramids."

New theory

By the Middle Ages, many Europeans could no longer accept the idea that the pyramids were tombs. Instead,

The Jewish historian known as Flavius Josephus argued in the 1st century AD that the pyramids were built by Hebrew slaves.

This beautiful mosaic in St. Mark's Cathedral in Venice, Italy, shows the pyramids as grain stores with windows and doors. Men bring wheat to fill them.

John Greaves *was the first person to produce accurate pictures of the pyramids. This page from his book* Pyramidographia *shows the entrance to the Great Pyramid.*

they looked to the Bible for an explanation of the pyramids. They found the answer in the story of great barns or granaries, built for a pharaoh by his chief official, Joseph.

Guide books

From the 16th century, European travelers visited Egypt and published illustrations and descriptions of the pyramids. These publications were the first guide books to the pyramids. This was long before cameras, so the artists usually relied on their memory, or other people's, when they drew pictures. The artworks are often inaccurate and bear little resemblance to real pyramids—their sides are sometimes shown at much too steep an angle.

"Some men say they are the tombs of great men in ancient times… [but] they are empty inside and tombs ought not to be so high."

The Travels of Sir John Mandeville, 1356

Detailed research

In 1646, John Greaves, an English mathematician, published *Pyramidographia*. Greaves had traveled to Egypt to examine the pyramids. He entered the Great Pyramid, where he found himself surrounded by bats "so ugly and so large, exceeding 1 foot [30 cm] in length." Despite the bats, he was able to measure many of the internal passages, and correctly concluded that this was a royal tomb after all. Not all of his findings were as accurate. He miscalculated the measurements for the base

of the pyramid because of all the accumulated debris around it. However, his book was hugely influential and sparked a new interest in the pyramids and ancient Egypt. Scientific study of the pyramids had begun.

With the invention *of printing in the 15th century, many books about foreign lands were published. The illustrators often got the pyramids' shape wrong. In this illustration from 1668, the pyramids look much too pointed.*

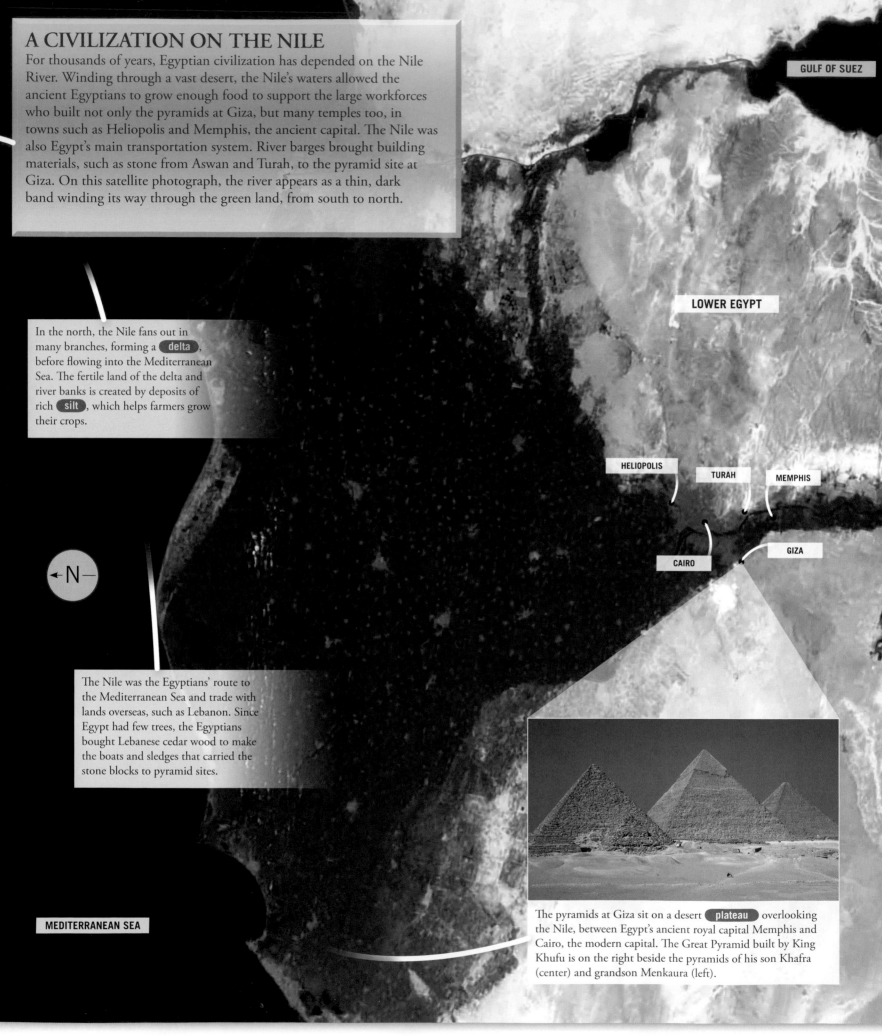

A CIVILIZATION ON THE NILE

For thousands of years, Egyptian civilization has depended on the Nile River. Winding through a vast desert, the Nile's waters allowed the ancient Egyptians to grow enough food to support the large workforces who built not only the pyramids at Giza, but many temples too, in towns such as Heliopolis and Memphis, the ancient capital. The Nile was also Egypt's main transportation system. River barges brought building materials, such as stone from Aswan and Turah, to the pyramid site at Giza. On this satellite photograph, the river appears as a thin, dark band winding its way through the green land, from south to north.

In the north, the Nile fans out in many branches, forming a **delta**, before flowing into the Mediterranean Sea. The fertile land of the delta and river banks is created by deposits of rich **silt**, which helps farmers grow their crops.

The Nile was the Egyptians' route to the Mediterranean Sea and trade with lands overseas, such as Lebanon. Since Egypt had few trees, the Egyptians bought Lebanese cedar wood to make the boats and sledges that carried the stone blocks to pyramid sites.

GULF OF SUEZ

LOWER EGYPT

HELIOPOLIS

TURAH

MEMPHIS

CAIRO

GIZA

← N →

MEDITERRANEAN SEA

The pyramids at Giza sit on a desert **plateau** overlooking the Nile, between Egypt's ancient royal capital Memphis and Cairo, the modern capital. The Great Pyramid built by King Khufu is on the right beside the pyramids of his son Khafra (center) and grandson Menkaura (left).

delta A triangular widening of a river into branches as it reaches the sea.

silt A mixture of mud and plant remains in river water that can build up on river banks and help to make land fertile.

plateau A wide, fairly flat piece of land that is higher than the land next to it.

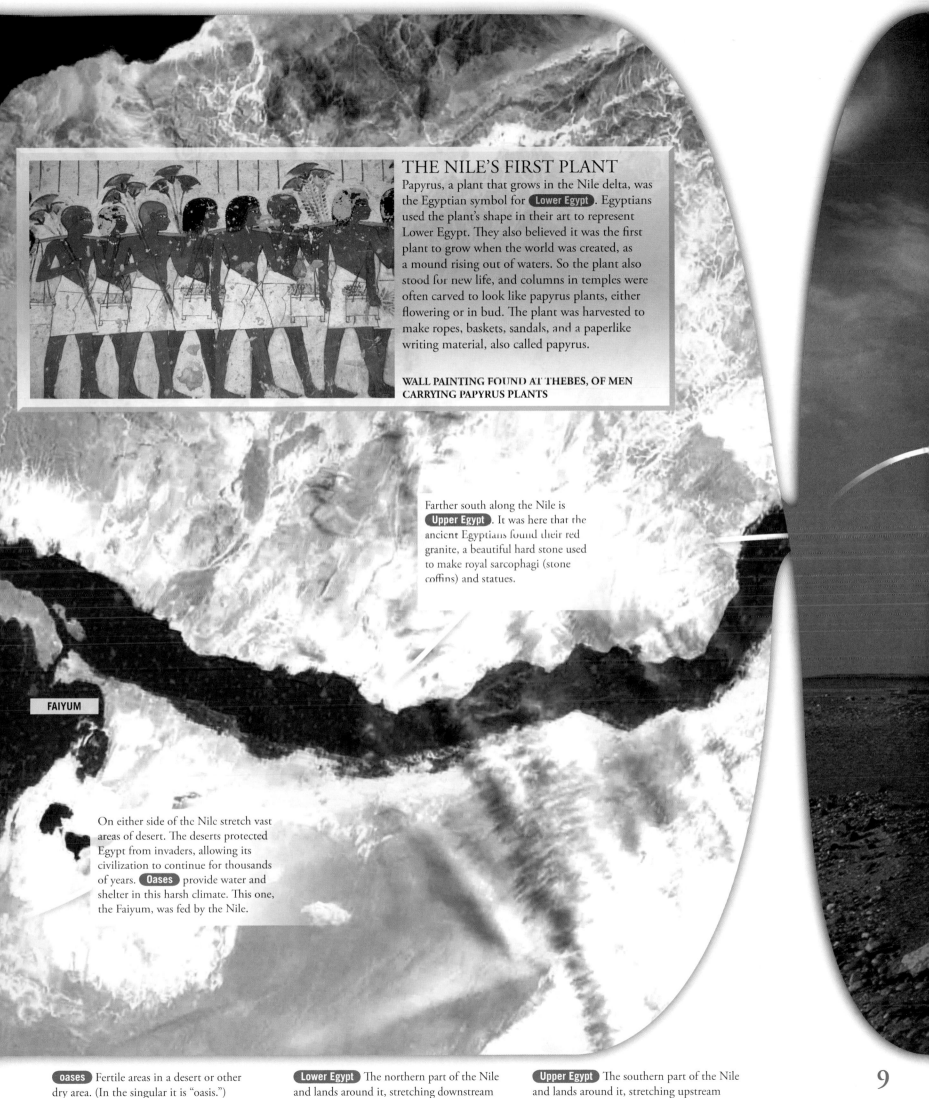

THE NILE'S FIRST PLANT

Papyrus, a plant that grows in the Nile delta, was the Egyptian symbol for **Lower Egypt**. Egyptians used the plant's shape in their art to represent Lower Egypt. They also believed it was the first plant to grow when the world was created, as a mound rising out of waters. So the plant also stood for new life, and columns in temples were often carved to look like papyrus plants, either flowering or in bud. The plant was harvested to make ropes, baskets, sandals, and a paperlike writing material, also called papyrus.

WALL PAINTING FOUND AT THEBES, OF MEN CARRYING PAPYRUS PLANTS

Farther south along the Nile is **Upper Egypt**. It was here that the ancient Egyptians found their red granite, a beautiful hard stone used to make royal sarcophagi (stone coffins) and statues.

FAIYUM

On either side of the Nile stretch vast areas of desert. The deserts protected Egypt from invaders, allowing its civilization to continue for thousands of years. **Oases** provide water and shelter in this harsh climate. This one, the Faiyum, was fed by the Nile.

oases Fertile areas in a desert or other dry area. (In the singular it is "oasis.")

Lower Egypt The northern part of the Nile and lands around it, stretching downstream from Memphis to the Mediterranean Sea.

Upper Egypt The southern part of the Nile and lands around it, stretching upstream from Memphis to modern-day Aswan.

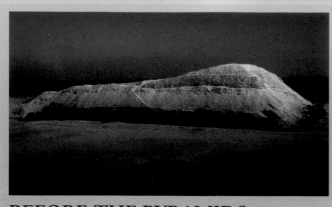

BEFORE THE PYRAMIDS

Pyramids developed from earlier tombs called mastabas. These were low buildings made of mud brick, and were designed to be palaces for the kings in their life after death. Then, some time around 2660 BC, King Djoser created a new type of tomb. By placing six mastabas of decreasing size one on top of another, he built the Step Pyramid.

King Snefru's first attempt to build a smooth-sided pyramid was at Meidum. The building started as a step pyramid, with smooth sides added later. That pyramid is now ruined. It was probably completed, but it was later robbed of its `casing stones`, as were most of the pyramids.

Inspired by Djoser, King Snefru had a new vision. He decided to build a pyramid with smooth sides. He made three attempts before he was happy with the result, seen here in the distance. This is King Snefru's North Pyramid at Dahshur.

King Snefru was the greatest pyramid-builder in history. He constructed three huge pyramids, containing a total of 124 million cubic feet (3.5 million cubic meters) of stone— 35 million more cubic feet than in the Great Pyramid of Giza.

STEP PYRAMID

King Djoser's Step Pyramid at Saqqara was the first large structure in the world to be made of stone rather than mud brick. The pharaoh must have wanted to build a tomb that could be seen for miles around and would last forever. The stepped levels were perhaps created to act as a gigantic stairway, helping the pharaoh's spirit climb up into the sky.

`casing stones` The outer layer of stones covering the pyramid, usually made from fine white limestone.

`foundation` The structure a building sits on, usually made from stone or from the hard rock of the ground.

Before builders finished the Bent Pyramid, work began on Snefru's North Pyramid. It was built with a gentler slope of 43° and horizontally laid stones. Its Egyptian name means "Shining Pyramid" and it could be the place where Snefru was buried.

King Snefru's next attempt was this pyramid, the Bent Pyramid at Dahshur. The lower part is smooth-sided with slopes at an angle of 54°. This steep angle meant that the pyramid was too heavy for its **foundation**. To lessen the load, the angle was reduced to 43° about halfway up, which is why the pyramid looks bent.

At the same time that the angle was changed, the builders began to lay the stones **horizontally**, instead of leaning inward. This made a more stable structure. With each new pyramid, the builders were finding out how to improve their designs.

FROM ARCHITECT TO GOD

The Step Pyramid was probably designed by Imhotep, King Djoser's vizier (chief minister) and **architect**. A royal statue lists Imhotep's many titles, including "first one under the king," "high priest," "chief sculptor," and "chief carpenter." Such was the respect for Imhotep's learning that later Egyptians worshiped him as a god of wisdom, writing, and medicine. They left small bronze statuettes of the architect as offerings in temples.

DETAIL FROM A STATUE OF IMHOTEP

horizontally Lying level or flat, parallel to the ground.

architect A person who designs buildings and oversees their construction.

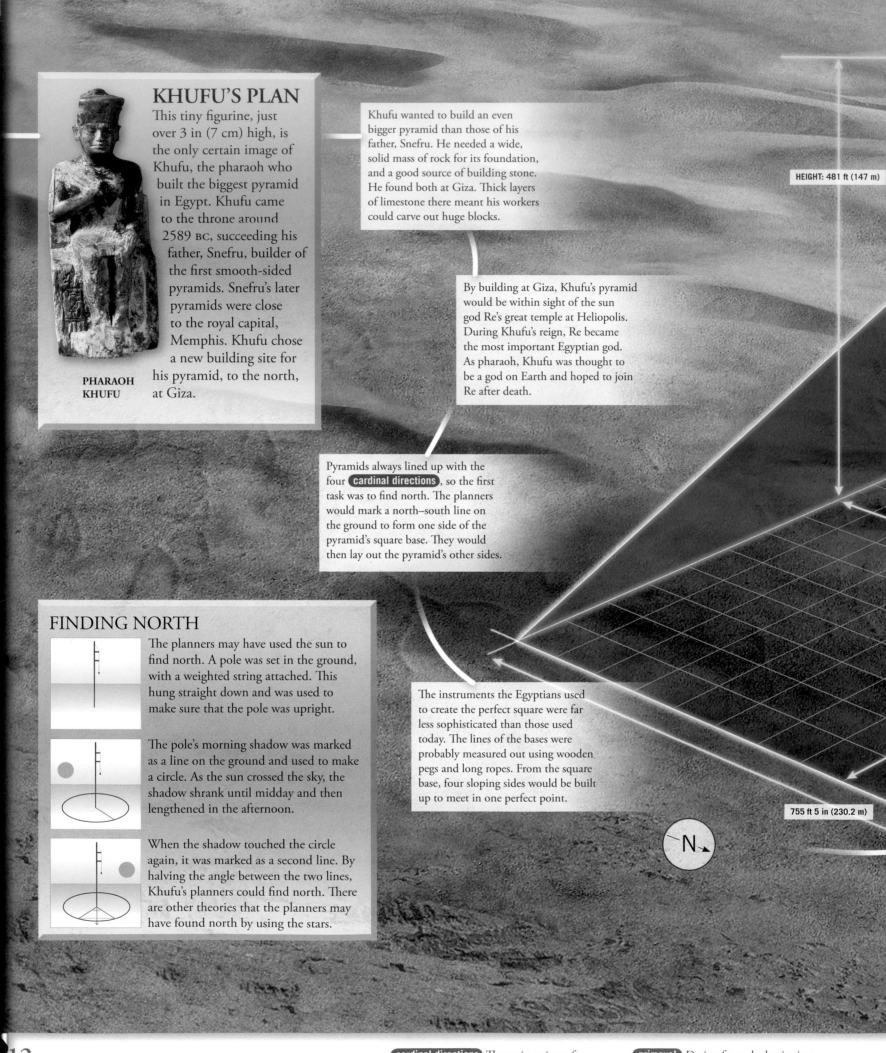

KHUFU'S PLAN

This tiny figurine, just over 3 in (7 cm) high, is the only certain image of Khufu, the pharaoh who built the biggest pyramid in Egypt. Khufu came to the throne around 2589 BC, succeeding his father, Snefru, builder of the first smooth-sided pyramids. Snefru's later pyramids were close to the royal capital, Memphis. Khufu chose a new building site for his pyramid, to the north, at Giza.

PHARAOH KHUFU

Khufu wanted to build an even bigger pyramid than those of his father, Snefru. He needed a wide, solid mass of rock for its foundation, and a good source of building stone. He found both at Giza. Thick layers of limestone there meant his workers could carve out huge blocks.

By building at Giza, Khufu's pyramid would be within sight of the sun god Re's great temple at Heliopolis. During Khufu's reign, Re became the most important Egyptian god. As pharaoh, Khufu was thought to be a god on Earth and hoped to join Re after death.

Pyramids always lined up with the four **cardinal directions**, so the first task was to find north. The planners would mark a north–south line on the ground to form one side of the pyramid's square base. They would then lay out the pyramid's other sides.

HEIGHT: 481 ft (147 m)

FINDING NORTH

The planners may have used the sun to find north. A pole was set in the ground, with a weighted string attached. This hung straight down and was used to make sure that the pole was upright.

The pole's morning shadow was marked as a line on the ground and used to make a circle. As the sun crossed the sky, the shadow shrank until midday and then lengthened in the afternoon.

When the shadow touched the circle again, it was marked as a second line. By halving the angle between the two lines, Khufu's planners could find north. There are other theories that the planners may have found north by using the stars.

The instruments the Egyptians used to create the perfect square were far less sophisticated than those used today. The lines of the bases were probably measured out using wooden pegs and long ropes. From the square base, four sloping sides would be built up to meet in one perfect point.

755 ft 5 in (230.2 m)

N

cardinal directions The main points of the compass: north, south, east, and west.

primeval Dating from the beginning of time.

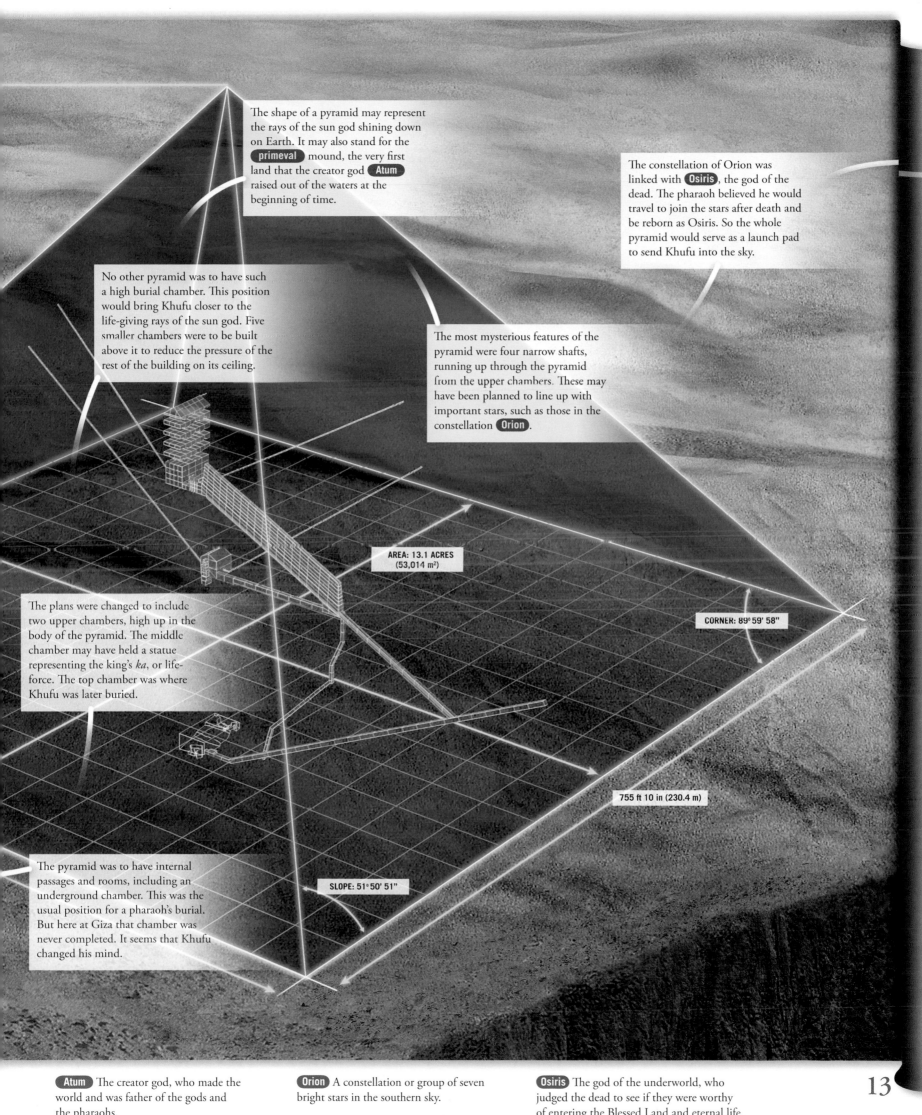

The shape of a pyramid may represent the rays of the sun god shining down on Earth. It may also stand for the **primeval** mound, the very first land that the creator god **Atum** raised out of the waters at the beginning of time.

The constellation of Orion was linked with **Osiris**, the god of the dead. The pharaoh believed he would travel to join the stars after death and be reborn as Osiris. So the whole pyramid would serve as a launch pad to send Khufu into the sky.

No other pyramid was to have such a high burial chamber. This position would bring Khufu closer to the life-giving rays of the sun god. Five smaller chambers were to be built above it to reduce the pressure of the rest of the building on its ceiling.

The most mysterious features of the pyramid were four narrow shafts, running up through the pyramid from the upper chambers. These may have been planned to line up with important stars, such as those in the constellation **Orion**.

The plans were changed to include two upper chambers, high up in the body of the pyramid. The middle chamber may have held a statue representing the king's *ka*, or life-force. The top chamber was where Khufu was later buried.

AREA: 13.1 ACRES (53,014 m²)

CORNER: 89° 59' 58"

755 ft 10 in (230.4 m)

SLOPE: 51° 50' 51"

The pyramid was to have internal passages and rooms, including an underground chamber. This was the usual position for a pharaoh's burial. But here at Giza that chamber was never completed. It seems that Khufu changed his mind.

Atum The creator god, who made the world and was father of the gods and the pharaohs.

Orion A constellation or group of seven bright stars in the southern sky.

Osiris The god of the underworld, who judged the dead to see if they were worthy of entering the Blessed Land and eternal life.

Most of the stone for Khufu's Great Pyramid came from a quarry 1,000 ft (300 m) to the south of the building site. The limestone here lies in very thick layers, which meant that large blocks could be cut from the quarry for the pyramid's core.

CUTTING GRANITE

Granite, the stone used for the pharaoh's burial chamber and sarcophagus (stone coffin), was too hard to be cut using copper tools. The only way that the quarrymen at Aswan could carve out granite blocks was with pear-shaped hammerstones made from diabase. This stone is even harder than granite, but eventually wears away with constant use.

QUARRYMAN WITH HAMMERSTONE, FROM A TOMB PAINTING AT SAQQARA

The workers' first task was to remove the sand and rubble from the desert's surface, revealing the limestone underneath. Then they marked out the outline of blocks in red ocher paint. Traces of this paint have been found on building blocks at Giza.

Using chisels and **mallets**, the men also cut slots around the base of each block. These were sockets for the wooden levers. A team of men around the block strained together on the levers until, with a great crack, it broke loose.

Using stone **picks** and copper-bladed **chisels**, the quarrymen hacked out channels around each block. These channels had to be wide, so that the men could then use long wooden **levers** to pry the blocks free from the stone beneath.

Workers cut down until they reached the softer stone lying between two layers of limestone, where it was easy to free a block. Because the size of the layers varied, so did the size of the blocks. The deeper the layer, the larger and heavier the block could be.

picks Tools with a sharp, pointed end, used to break rock or hard soil.

chisels Tools with a sharp cutting edge at one end, used to chip away stone.

levers Long wooden bars used to help lift a load. One end of a lever is put under the load and the other is pulled or pushed down.

SHINING STONE

The coarse texture and dull color of Giza limestone made it unsuitable for the pyramid's `casing`, which Khufu wanted to shine like the sun. Instead, the builders used fine white limestone from Turah, on the east side of the Nile. This limestone lies under layers of coarser stone, so the quarrymen had to tunnel to reach it, cutting into and under the rock face.

TURAH QUARRY

In 1992, Egyptologist Mark Lehner built a miniature pyramid as an experiment. He estimates that there must have been about 1,200 men working at Giza to quarry enough stone to build the pyramid in the pharaoh's 23-year reign.

By the time the pyramid was completed, more than two million blocks had been quarried at Giza, and the quarry floor lay 100 ft (30 m) below the original surface. Almost 98 million cu ft (three million m³) of stone had been removed.

Fortunately, the Egyptians had plenty of experience of moving heavy stone, from building the earlier pyramids. Their teams of men must have been well organized—they needed to keep a constant flow of blocks coming from the quarry to the building site.

Once a block was cut free, a team of workers had to heave it onto a slatted wooden `sledge`. These blocks were heavy, with an average weight of 2.5 tons. There were no wheels or cranes to help—all the men had were levers and ropes.

`mallets` Hammers with a large head, made of stone, wood, or metal. Mallets may have been used to hammer chisels.

`sledge` A carrier that uses runners instead of wheels to move heavy loads. The Egyptians had not yet discovered the wheel.

`casing` The outer layer of stones covering the pyramid. They were made of fine white limestone and polished to shine in the sun.

Working alongside the quarrymen were teams of haulers. They spent long hours under the blistering-hot sun, dragging sledges loaded with heavy blocks up to the building site. A team of 20 men could move perhaps ten blocks a day at first, down to five as the pyramid grew higher.

The workers built a hard roadway to support the constant stream of heavily loaded sledges. They set wooden beams in the ground and packed the spaces in between with stone chips and **mortar**. This stopped the sledges from sinking into the sand.

Archaeologists have discovered a hauling trackway at Lisht, near a later pyramid. It was made from timbers of Lebanese cedar, which probably came from an old **barge**. Wood was a scarce resource in Egypt, which is why it was often reused for a different purpose.

To build the pyramid, 340 blocks a day had to be hauled out of the quarry. This could have been done by around 1,400 men, working in 70 teams. There must have been **foremen** directing the teams, taking their orders from higher officials.

The haulers pulled the sledges with ropes made from plant fibers, including hemp and papyrus. Archaeologists have found ancient ropes of various thicknesses, including some strong enough to pull weights of up to five tons. Ropemakers were yet another group of workers who helped to build the pyramid.

BAD BACKS

In 1990, archaeologist Zahi Hawass discovered a cemetery where many of the people who worked at Giza were buried. Their skeletons showed that they were well cared for, with signs of medical treatment, such as broken bones that had been set. However, the majority suffered from bad backs, due to heavy physical labor.

mortar A mixture of materials, usually including sand and water, used to bond stones together.

barge A flat-bottomed boat used mainly to transport goods. On the Nile, barges were used to bring stone for the pyramid.

foremen The men responsible for organizing the workers. There may have been one foreman for each gang of 20 men.

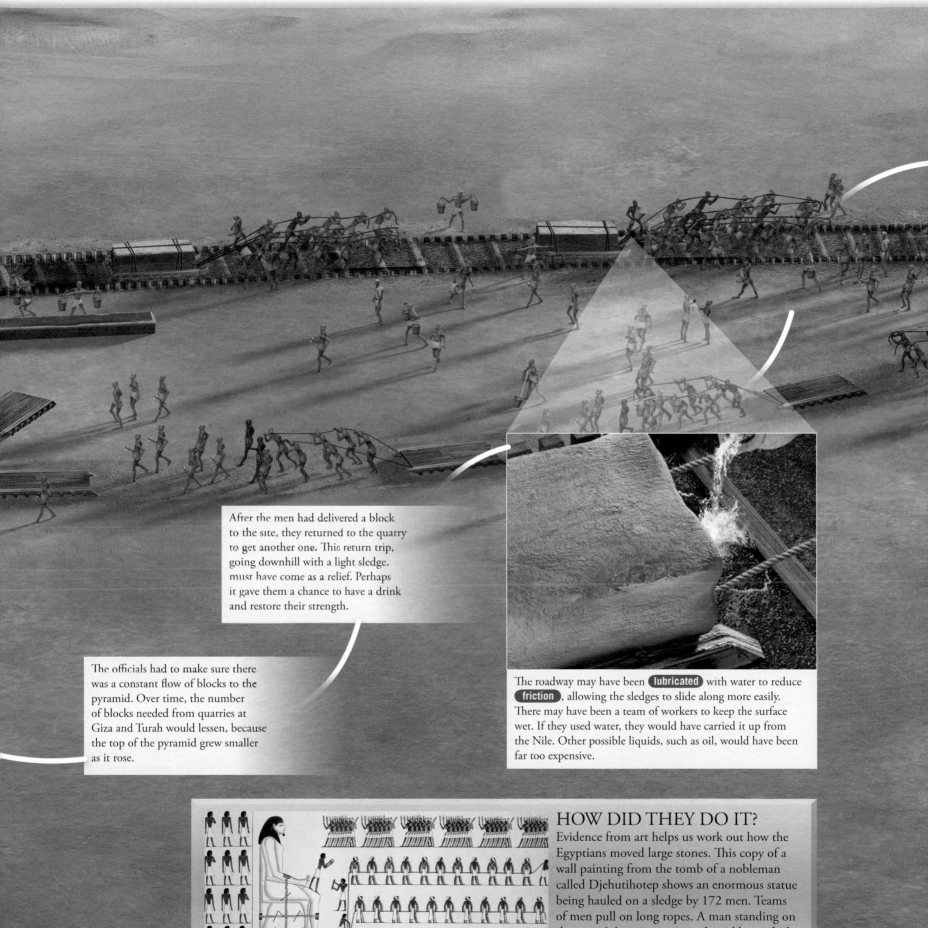

After the men had delivered a block to the site, they returned to the quarry to get another one. This return trip, going downhill with a light sledge, must have come as a relief. Perhaps it gave them a chance to have a drink and restore their strength.

The officials had to make sure there was a constant flow of blocks to the pyramid. Over time, the number of blocks needed from quarries at Giza and Turah would lessen, because the top of the pyramid grew smaller as it rose.

The roadway may have been **lubricated** with water to reduce **friction**, allowing the sledges to slide along more easily. There may have been a team of workers to keep the surface wet. If they used water, they would have carried it up from the Nile. Other possible liquids, such as oil, would have been far too expensive.

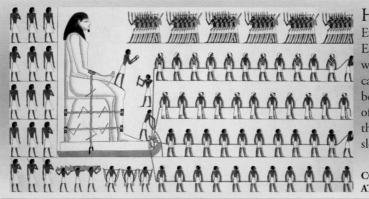

HOW DID THEY DO IT?

Evidence from art helps us work out how the Egyptians moved large stones. This copy of a wall painting from the tomb of a nobleman called Djehutihotep shows an enormous statue being hauled on a sledge by 172 men. Teams of men pull on long ropes. A man standing on the statue's base is pouring a liquid beneath the sledge runners to help the sledge slide forward.

COPY MADE BY FREDERIC CAILLAUD, c. 1820, AT EL-BERSHEH

lubricated Covered with water or another substance to make a surface smooth and slippery.

friction One object rubbing against another. The greater the friction, the more effort it takes to move a heavy load.

After dragging their heavy sledges along a hauling track, the workers finally reached the building site, which was just as busy as the quarry. Here, more teams of workers were **leveling** the ground. The ground needed to be level so that level layers of stone could be placed in position.

Rather than flatten the whole site, with its area of over 538,000 sq ft (50,000 square meters), the planners decided to leave the central **bedrock** within the pyramid. A wide strip around the edges of the bedrock was leveled and used to build the **foundation** platform.

THE OVERSEER

The pharaoh's nephew, Hemiunu, was the man in charge of the whole project. On the base of his statue, he is described as "overseer of all construction projects to the king." The statue was found in his tomb, next to the pyramid he had built for his uncle.

STATUE OF HEMIUNU

Before work had even begun on the site, **surveyors** set out a straight line of posts linked by cords around each side of the pyramid. This acted as a reference line. By measuring a set distance inside the line, the builders knew exactly where the edges of the pyramid should lie.

leveling Flattening the ground in preparation for a new building.

bedrock The strong, solid rock that lies under soil and surface rock.

foundation The base that supports a building and stops it from sinking into the ground.

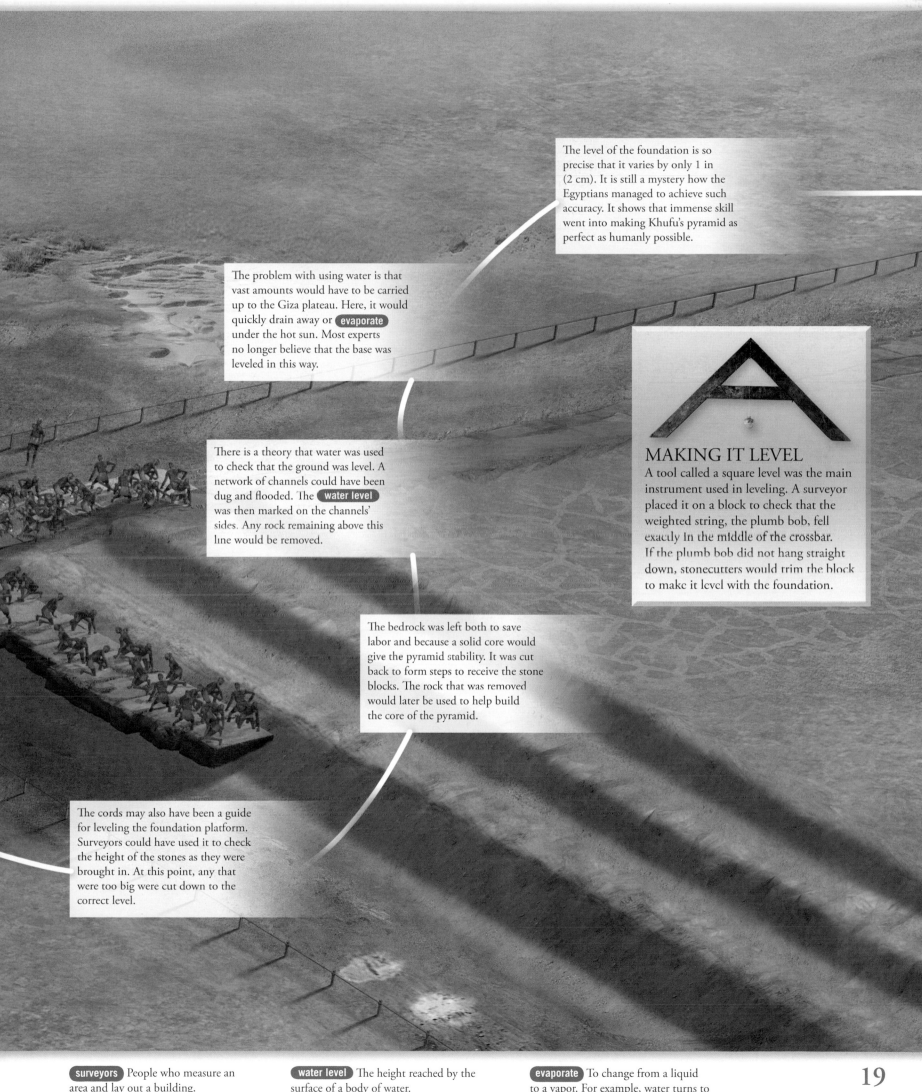

The level of the foundation is so precise that it varies by only 1 in (2 cm). It is still a mystery how the Egyptians managed to achieve such accuracy. It shows that immense skill went into making Khufu's pyramid as perfect as humanly possible.

The problem with using water is that vast amounts would have to be carried up to the Giza plateau. Here, it would quickly drain away or evaporate under the hot sun. Most experts no longer believe that the base was leveled in this way.

There is a theory that water was used to check that the ground was level. A network of channels could have been dug and flooded. The water level was then marked on the channels' sides. Any rock remaining above this line would be removed.

MAKING IT LEVEL

A tool called a square level was the main instrument used in leveling. A surveyor placed it on a block to check that the weighted string, the plumb bob, fell exactly in the middle of the crossbar. If the plumb bob did not hang straight down, stonecutters would trim the block to make it level with the foundation.

The bedrock was left both to save labor and because a solid core would give the pyramid stability. It was cut back to form steps to receive the stone blocks. The rock that was removed would later be used to help build the core of the pyramid.

The cords may also have been a guide for leveling the foundation platform. Surveyors could have used it to check the height of the stones as they were brought in. At this point, any that were too big were cut down to the correct level.

---

surveyors People who measure an area and lay out a building.

water level The height reached by the surface of a body of water.

evaporate To change from a liquid to a vapor. For example, water turns to steam when heated.

CATALOG OF TOOLS

Building a pyramid was a complex task, but the tools the Egyptians used were very simple. In the time of Khufu, the Egyptians had not yet learned how to make objects from the harder metals, such as bronze or iron. Instead, they depended on stone pounders and on chisels and drills with relatively soft, copper blades. To measure angles and distances, they used plant-fiber ropes, wooden rods, and wooden set squares.

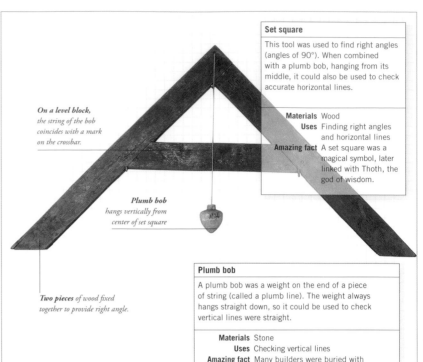

Set square

This tool was used to find right angles (angles of 90°). When combined with a plumb bob, hanging from its middle, it could also be used to check accurate horizontal lines.

Materials	Wood
Uses	Finding right angles and horizontal lines
Amazing fact	A set square was a magical symbol, later linked with Thoth, the god of wisdom.

On a level block, the string of the bob coincides with a mark on the crossbar.

Plumb bob hangs vertically from center of set square

Two pieces of wood fixed together to provide right angle.

Chisel

Chisels were made from copper—a metal that was mined in the eastern desert. Copper is a fairly soft metal, so the chisels would quickly become blunt with repeated chipping against stone. They required frequent sharpening. In addition, their blades also had to be very narrow, because wide blades bend when struck on stone.

Materials	Copper
Uses	Shaping stone and carving inscriptions
Amazing fact	For all its vast size, the Great Pyramid was finished using chisels as narrow as a thumb.

End of chisel needed regular sharpening

Rounded end struck by mallet

Plumb bob

A plumb bob was a weight on the end of a piece of string (called a plumb line). The weight always hangs straight down, so it could be used to check vertical lines were straight.

Materials	Stone
Uses	Checking vertical lines
Amazing fact	Many builders were buried with plumb bobs or other tools to use in the afterlife.

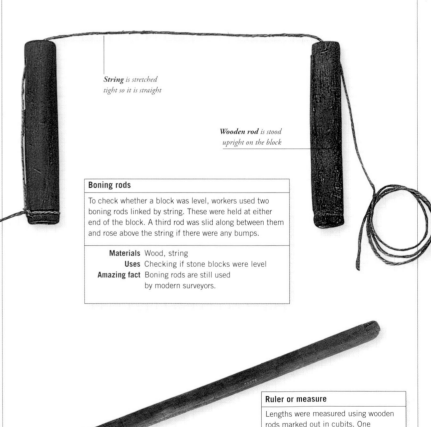

String is stretched tight so it is straight

Wooden rod is stood upright on the block

Mallet

The stonecutter struck his chisel with a mallet, held in the other hand. Egyptian mallets were made of wood. The head of this mallet has been worn away by constant use.

Materials	Wood
Uses	Striking a chisel to cut stone
Amazing fact	This mallet was found in the tomb of an Egyptian architect named Kha and dates from about 1405 BC.

Short handle is carved for a better grip

Boning rods

To check whether a block was level, workers used two boning rods linked by string. These were held at either end of the block. A third rod was slid along between them and rose above the string if there were any bumps.

Materials	Wood, string
Uses	Checking if stone blocks were level
Amazing fact	Boning rods are still used by modern surveyors.

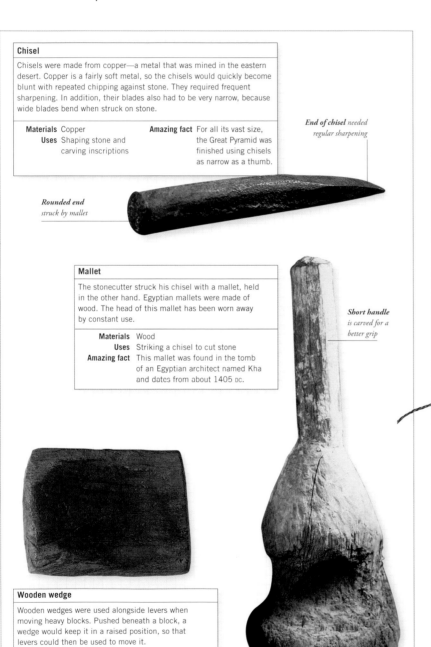

Wooden wedge

Wooden wedges were used alongside levers when moving heavy blocks. Pushed beneath a block, a wedge would keep it in a raised position, so that levers could then be used to move it.

Materials	Wood
Uses	Propping blocks
Amazing fact	The wedge shown here is more than 3,000 years old.

Rod is marked with measurements called digits and palms—there were four digits in a palm and seven palms in a cubit

Ruler or measure

Lengths were measured using wooden rods marked out in cubits. One cubit equaled the length of a man's forearm—about 21 in (52 cm).

Materials	Wood
Uses	Measuring length
Amazing fact	We still have units of measurement based on the human body—in our case, feet!

Scaffolding

We know from tomb paintings that the Egyptians used scaffolding—wooden poles tied together with ropes made of plant material. Scaffolding was probably built out of short lengths of locally grown acacia wood.

Yoke

Goods of all kinds were carried by being slung from a long pole, resting on the shoulders, called a yoke. The men in this wall painting are carrying stone blocks. The yoke was moved across the shoulders until the blocks balanced.

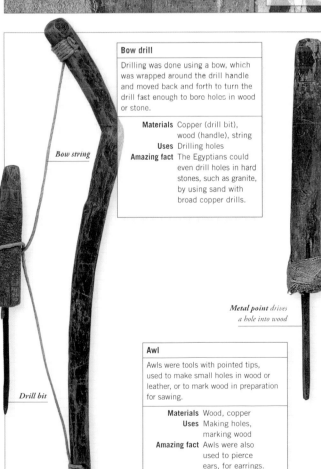

Bow string

Bow drill

Drilling was done using a bow, which was wrapped around the drill handle and moved back and forth to turn the drill fast enough to bore holes in wood or stone.

Materials Copper (drill bit), wood (handle), string
Uses Drilling holes
Amazing fact The Egyptians could even drill holes in hard stones, such as granite, by using sand with broad copper drills.

Wooden handle

Copper saw

A copper-bladed saw could be used to cut wood, or with sand to cut stone—the saw moved the grains of sand, which did the actual cutting.

Materials Wood, copper
Uses Cutting wood or stones
Amazing fact Egyptian saws were pulled rather than pushed.

Metal point drives a hole into wood

Awl

Awls were tools with pointed tips, used to make small holes in wood or leather, or to mark wood in preparation for sawing.

Materials Wood, copper
Uses Making holes, marking wood
Amazing fact Awls were also used to pierce ears, for earrings.

Drill bit

Cutting edge

Basket

Building materials, tools, debris, and food were all carried in baskets. Baskets were also the most common items in any Egyptian home. Since wood for storage chests was scarce, most people kept all their belongings in baskets.

Materials Plant fibers, such as palm leaves
Uses Carrying and storage
Amazing fact The Egyptians made baskets long before they learned to make pottery.

Basket woven using strips of plant fibers

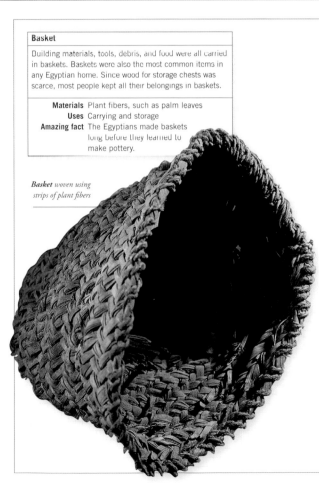

RIVER TRANSPORTATION

The Nile River, Egypt's main transportation corridor, played a central role in the building of Khufu's pyramid. It carried workers and supplies from farms throughout the land to the building site. The river was also used to transport granite, a stone highly prized for its strength and beauty, which was needed for the pharaoh's burial chamber and sarcophagus. Barges brought this stone from Aswan, over 560 miles (900 km) south of Giza. They also brought fine limestone from Turah, located across the river.

The granite quarries at Aswan lie to the east of the island of Elephantine. This island is just to the north of the first **cataract** in the Nile, which formed the natural southern boundary of the Egyptian kingdom during ancient times.

Once the blocks were safely loaded and secured onboard, the barge began its voyage **downriver**. Although the current helped push the barge along, it may also have been powered by oars. Large oars at the back of the boats were used for steering.

The granite blocks were brought to the river on sledges. The slabs used in the burial chamber are over 18 ft (5.5 m) long and weigh up to 45 tons. The workmen needed bigger sledges than the ones used to move limestone blocks at Giza, and each sledge would have had a large team of haulers.

How such massive stones were moved onto barges without capsizing the boats remains a mystery. The workmen might have built an earthen **embankment** alongside the barge and dragged the slabs slowly and carefully on board.

cataract Area of rapids in a river. These formed the southern boundary of Egypt.

embankment Raised area of a river bank, used to help boats dock.

downriver The direction in which the current of a river runs, from source to sea.

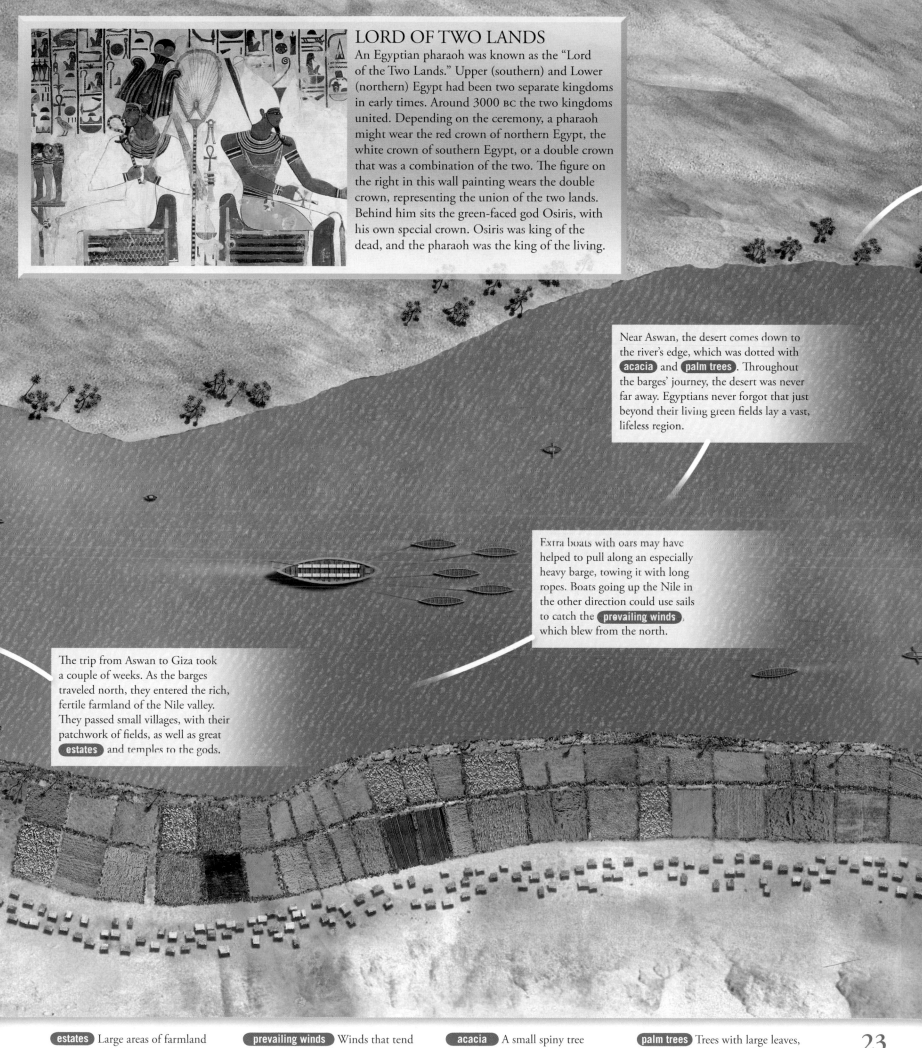

LORD OF TWO LANDS

An Egyptian pharaoh was known as the "Lord of the Two Lands." Upper (southern) and Lower (northern) Egypt had been two separate kingdoms in early times. Around 3000 BC the two kingdoms united. Depending on the ceremony, a pharaoh might wear the red crown of northern Egypt, the white crown of southern Egypt, or a double crown that was a combination of the two. The figure on the right in this wall painting wears the double crown, representing the union of the two lands. Behind him sits the green-faced god Osiris, with his own special crown. Osiris was king of the dead, and the pharaoh was the king of the living.

Near Aswan, the desert comes down to the river's edge, which was dotted with **acacia** and **palm trees**. Throughout the barges' journey, the desert was never far away. Egyptians never forgot that just beyond their living green fields lay a vast, lifeless region.

Extra boats with oars may have helped to pull along an especially heavy barge, towing it with long ropes. Boats going up the Nile in the other direction could use sails to catch the **prevailing winds**, which blew from the north.

The trip from Aswan to Giza took a couple of weeks. As the barges traveled north, they entered the rich, fertile farmland of the Nile valley. They passed small villages, with their patchwork of fields, as well as great **estates** and temples to the gods.

estates Large areas of farmland owned by the pharaoh, noblemen, or temples.

prevailing winds Winds that tend always to blow in the same direction.

acacia A small spiny tree common in Egypt, with a twisting trunk and branches.

palm trees Trees with large leaves, cultivated for their fruit (called dates), leaves, and husks.

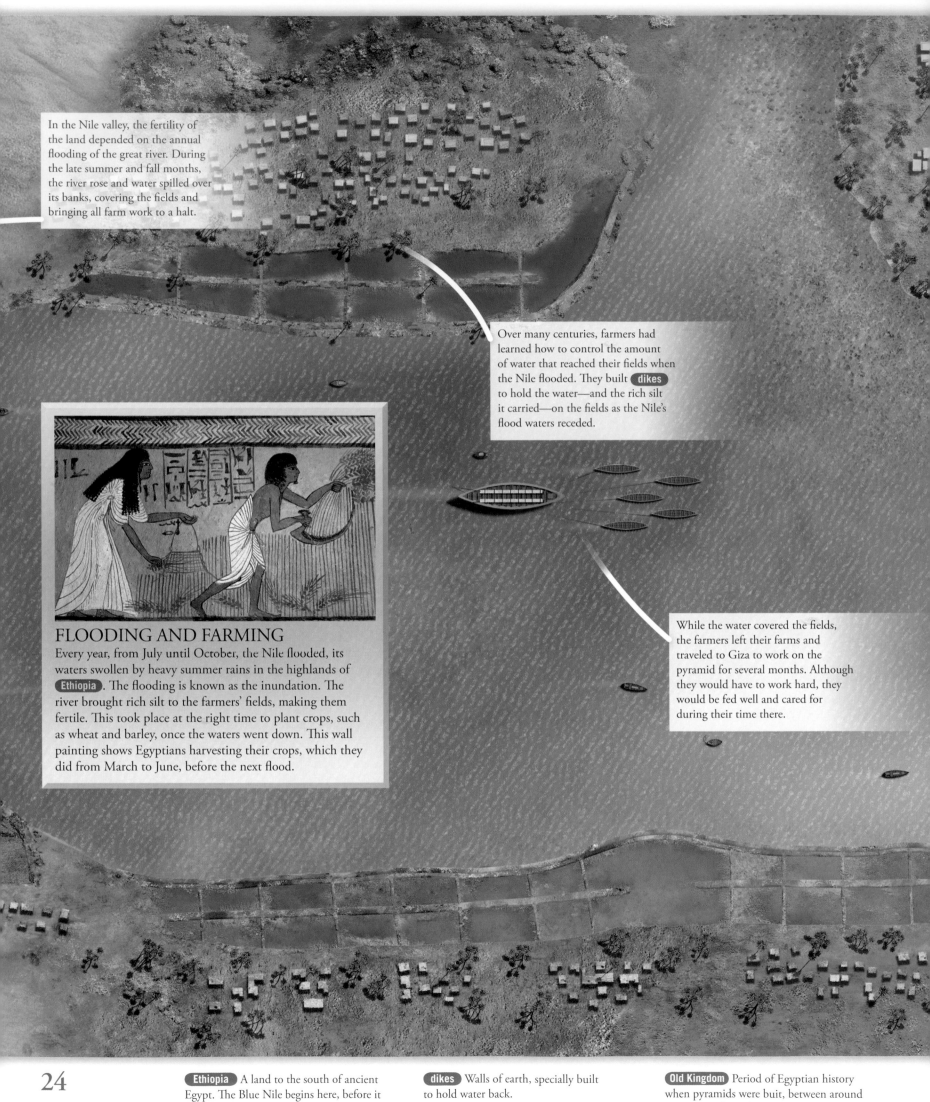

In the Nile valley, the fertility of the land depended on the annual flooding of the great river. During the late summer and fall months, the river rose and water spilled over its banks, covering the fields and bringing all farm work to a halt.

Over many centuries, farmers had learned how to control the amount of water that reached their fields when the Nile flooded. They built dikes to hold the water—and the rich silt it carried—on the fields as the Nile's flood waters receded.

FLOODING AND FARMING

Every year, from July until October, the Nile flooded, its waters swollen by heavy summer rains in the highlands of Ethiopia. The flooding is known as the inundation. The river brought rich silt to the farmers' fields, making them fertile. This took place at the right time to plant crops, such as wheat and barley, once the waters went down. This wall painting shows Egyptians harvesting their crops, which they did from March to June, before the next flood.

While the water covered the fields, the farmers left their farms and traveled to Giza to work on the pyramid for several months. Although they would have to work hard, they would be fed well and cared for during their time there.

Ethiopia A land to the south of ancient Egypt. The Blue Nile begins here, before it joins the White Nile to form the great river.

dikes Walls of earth, specially built to hold water back.

Old Kingdom Period of Egyptian history when pyramids were built, between around 2630 BC and 2134 BC.

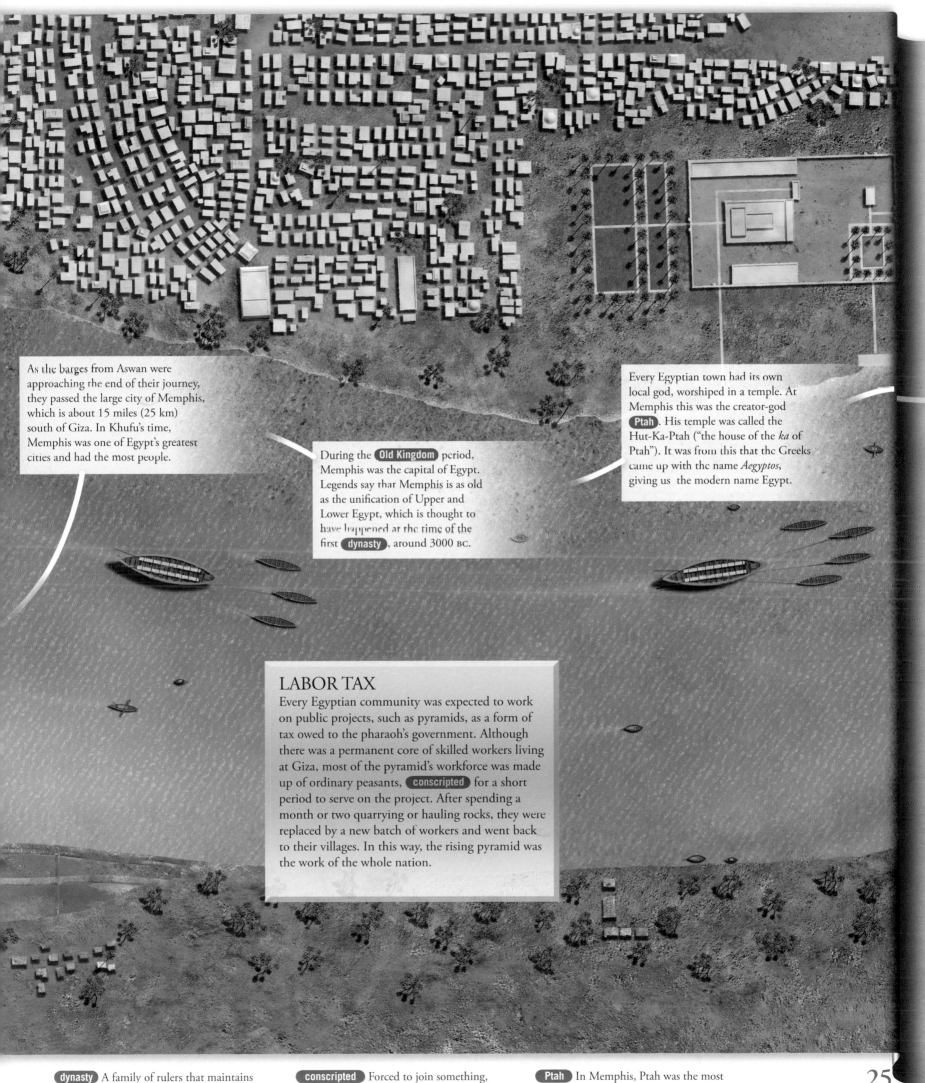

As the barges from Aswan were approaching the end of their journey, they passed the large city of Memphis, which is about 15 miles (25 km) south of Giza. In Khufu's time, Memphis was one of Egypt's greatest cities and had the most people.

During the **Old Kingdom** period, Memphis was the capital of Egypt. Legends say that Memphis is as old as the unification of Upper and Lower Egypt, which is thought to have happened at the time of the first **dynasty**, around 3000 BC.

Every Egyptian town had its own local god, worshiped in a temple. At Memphis this was the creator-god **Ptah**. His temple was called the Hut-Ka-Ptah ("the house of the *ka* of Ptah"). It was from this that the Greeks came up with the name *Aegyptos*, giving us the modern name Egypt.

LABOR TAX

Every Egyptian community was expected to work on public projects, such as pyramids, as a form of tax owed to the pharaoh's government. Although there was a permanent core of skilled workers living at Giza, most of the pyramid's workforce was made up of ordinary peasants, **conscripted** for a short period to serve on the project. After spending a month or two quarrying or hauling rocks, they were replaced by a new batch of workers and went back to their villages. In this way, the rising pyramid was the work of the whole nation.

dynasty A family of rulers that maintains power over a long period of time.

conscripted Forced to join something, such as an army or workforce, whether willing or not.

Ptah In Memphis, Ptah was the most important of all gods. He was the patron god of artisans and craftsmen.

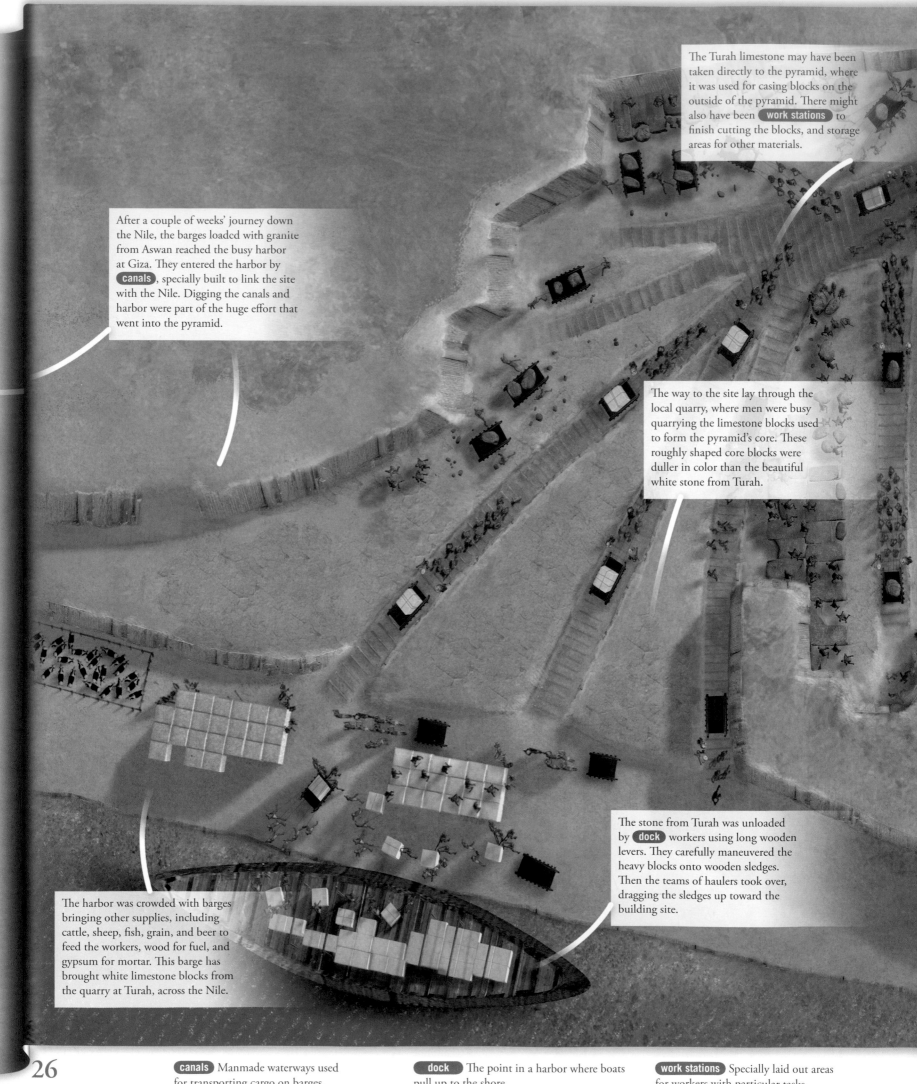

The Turah limestone may have been taken directly to the pyramid, where it was used for casing blocks on the outside of the pyramid. There might also have been **work stations** to finish cutting the blocks, and storage areas for other materials.

After a couple of weeks' journey down the Nile, the barges loaded with granite from Aswan reached the busy harbor at Giza. They entered the harbor by **canals**, specially built to link the site with the Nile. Digging the canals and harbor were part of the huge effort that went into the pyramid.

The way to the site lay through the local quarry, where men were busy quarrying the limestone blocks used to form the pyramid's core. These roughly shaped core blocks were duller in color than the beautiful white stone from Turah.

The stone from Turah was unloaded by **dock** workers using long wooden levers. They carefully maneuvered the heavy blocks onto wooden sledges. Then the teams of haulers took over, dragging the sledges up toward the building site.

The harbor was crowded with barges bringing other supplies, including cattle, sheep, fish, grain, and beer to feed the workers, wood for fuel, and gypsum for mortar. This barge has brought white limestone blocks from the quarry at Turah, across the Nile.

canals Manmade waterways used for transporting cargo on barges.

dock The point in a harbor where boats pull up to the shore.

work stations Specially laid out areas for workers with particular tasks.

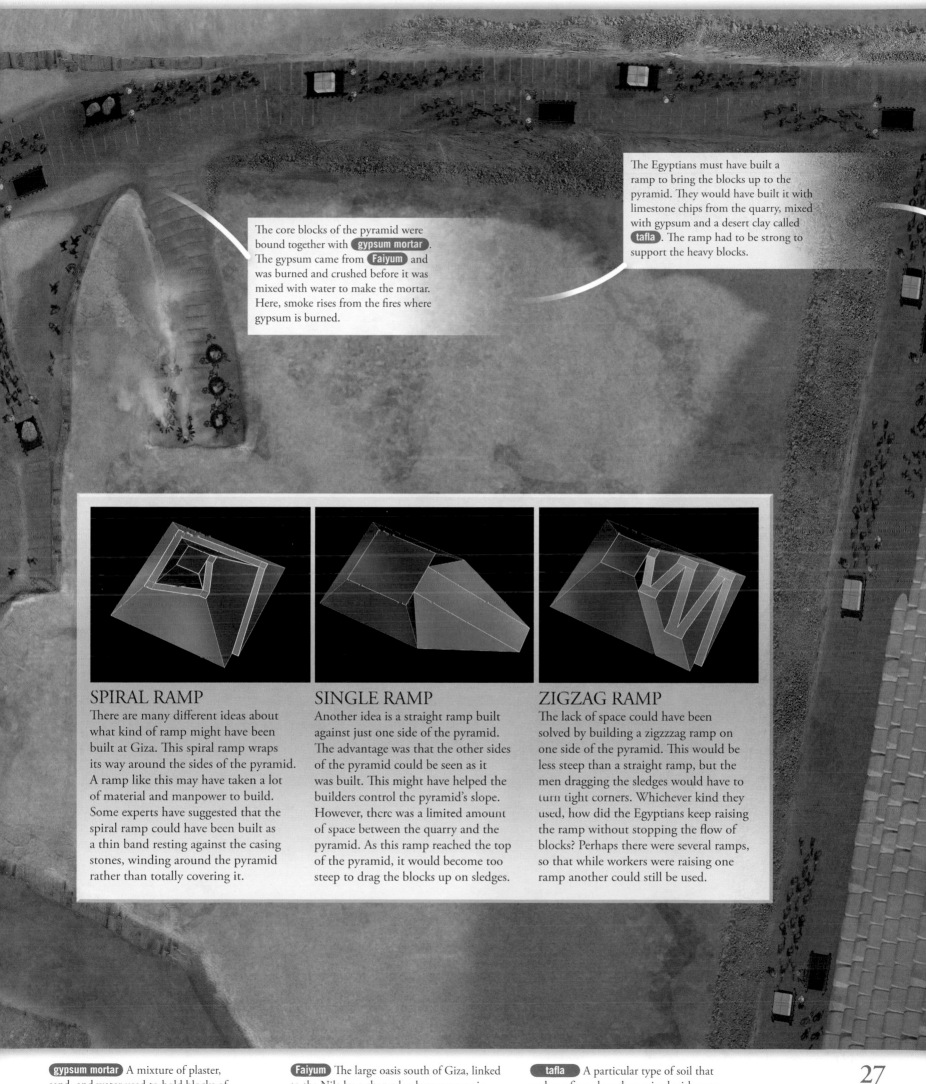

The core blocks of the pyramid were bound together with **gypsum mortar**. The gypsum came from **Faiyum** and was burned and crushed before it was mixed with water to make the mortar. Here, smoke rises from the fires where gypsum is burned.

The Egyptians must have built a ramp to bring the blocks up to the pyramid. They would have built it with limestone chips from the quarry, mixed with gypsum and a desert clay called **tafla**. The ramp had to be strong to support the heavy blocks.

SPIRAL RAMP

There are many different ideas about what kind of ramp might have been built at Giza. This spiral ramp wraps its way around the sides of the pyramid. A ramp like this may have taken a lot of material and manpower to build. Some experts have suggested that the spiral ramp could have been built as a thin band resting against the casing stones, winding around the pyramid rather than totally covering it.

SINGLE RAMP

Another idea is a straight ramp built against just one side of the pyramid. The advantage was that the other sides of the pyramid could be seen as it was built. This might have helped the builders control the pyramid's slope. However, there was a limited amount of space between the quarry and the pyramid. As this ramp reached the top of the pyramid, it would become too steep to drag the blocks up on sledges.

ZIGZAG RAMP

The lack of space could have been solved by building a zigzzzag ramp on one side of the pyramid. This would be less steep than a straight ramp, but the men dragging the sledges would have to turn tight corners. Whichever kind they used, how did the Egyptians keep raising the ramp without stopping the flow of blocks? Perhaps there were several ramps, so that while workers were raising one ramp another could still be used.

gypsum mortar A mixture of plaster, sand, and water used to hold blocks of stone together.

Faiyum The large oasis south of Giza, linked to the Nile by a channel, where gypsum is still found today.

tafla A particular type of soil that makes a firm clay when mixed with water.

27

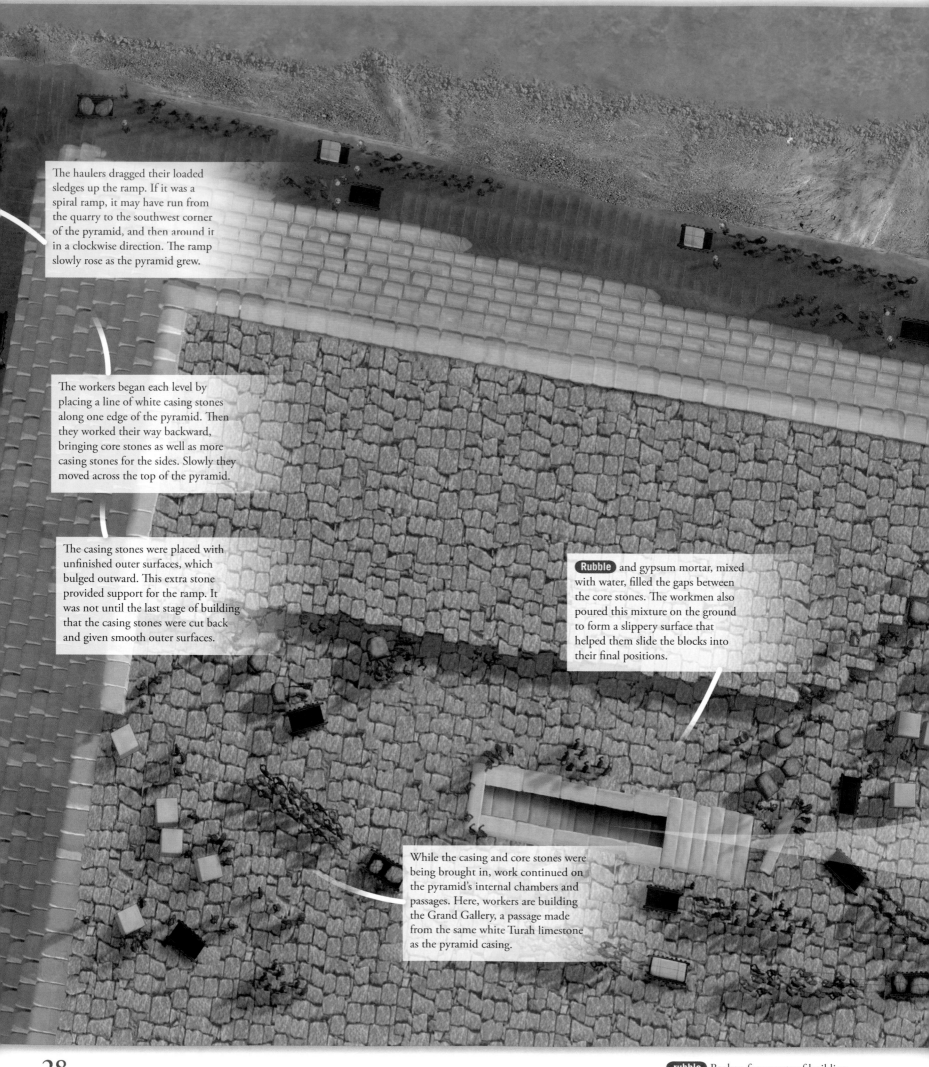

The haulers dragged their loaded sledges up the ramp. If it was a spiral ramp, it may have run from the quarry to the southwest corner of the pyramid, and then around it in a clockwise direction. The ramp slowly rose as the pyramid grew.

The workers began each level by placing a line of white casing stones along one edge of the pyramid. Then they worked their way backward, bringing core stones as well as more casing stones for the sides. Slowly they moved across the top of the pyramid.

The casing stones were placed with unfinished outer surfaces, which bulged outward. This extra stone provided support for the ramp. It was not until the last stage of building that the casing stones were cut back and given smooth outer surfaces.

Rubble and gypsum mortar, mixed with water, filled the gaps between the core stones. The workmen also poured this mixture on the ground to form a slippery surface that helped them slide the blocks into their final positions.

While the casing and core stones were being brought in, work continued on the pyramid's internal chambers and passages. Here, workers are building the Grand Gallery, a passage made from the same white Turah limestone as the pyramid casing.

rubble Broken fragments of building material, such as stone.

LIVING ON SITE

The workers who built the pyramid lived in their own town at Giza. Here there were mud-brick dwellings for the permanent workers and their families, and buildings like **barracks** for the temporary workforce. Egyptologist Mark Lehner has discovered a food-processing area with granaries, bakeries, and workshops for making tools and pottery. These areas are still being **excavated** and more information about the workers' daily lives is continually being uncovered. For example, bones of fish, geese, pigeons, and cows show that the workers had a good diet.

Each level of the pyramid had a smaller working surface than the level beneath, and so fewer blocks and workers were needed over time. It took the builders much longer to build the lower levels than those higher up.

As the pyramid rose, the internal chambers and passages took shape. The largest was the Grand Gallery, which was long and narrow. Constructed at a steep angle, this needed a great deal more skill to build than the surrounding core. The Gallery linked the narrower ascending passage with the upper burial chamber, which was not yet built.

barracks Large building where workers or soldiers are housed.

excavate To remove soil and rubble to reveal objects and structures beneath.

GRAND GALLERY

The Grand Gallery led up to Khufu's burial chamber, just beyond a small entrance at the far end. This was part of the pyramid's security system. It was a storage space for huge granite plugs, which were released after the funeral to slide down the ascending passage and block it. This was the only pyramid built to be sealed from the inside. It had to be done this way because the burial chamber is so high up. All other pyramids have low burial chambers, which could be sealed by dropping blocks in from the outside.

Because of the corbeling, the two walls grew closer and closer together as they rose. The space at the top is just 3½ ft (1 m) wide—small enough to be spanned by a single row of slabs. These slabs rested in notches carved into the top of the walls.

Corbeling was first used in the pyramids of Khufu's father, Snefru, but only for the ceilings of his burial chambers. Khufu's Grand Gallery was the first use of corbeling on a large scale. It is one of the greatest achievements of ancient architecture.

The height of the Gallery was achieved thanks to corbeling. There are nine rows of blocks, made from white Turah limestone. The first two rows rise straight up. Each of the upper seven rows juts out 3 in (7.5 cm) over the one beneath.

The Grand Gallery is a vast structure, 153 ft (46.7 m) long, 28½ ft (8.7 m) high, and 6½ ft (2.1 m) wide at the bottom. This dark corridor rises through the pyramid's core. To see inside, we have made one wall transparent—its blocks are outlined in white.

At the bottom of the gallery, there is an entrance to a deep shaft. This was the escape route for the men who sealed the ascending passage after the pharaoh's funeral. It led to the descending corridor, which they could use to leave the pyramid.

ascending passage The route that leads from the descending corridor up to the burial chamber.

shaft A steep, narrow passageway.

descending corridor The route or passageway that leads from the pyramid entrance to the underground chamber.

The Grand Gallery rises at an angle of 26°, which is the same as the angle of the ascending passage. The gallery had to be at such a steep angle so that when the granite blocks were released, they would slide all the way down to the bottom.

At the bottom of the walls, there are stone ramps. Like the walls just above them, they are carved with mysterious slots—perhaps sockets for wooden beams. Such beams were probably used to hold back the granite plugs until it was time to release them.

The granite plugs were slightly wider than the lowest part of the ascending passage. This meant that they would slide almost to the bottom of the passage, where they would become stuck fast. Three granite plugs are still there today.

There are many theories about how the granite plugs were stored in the gallery. One possibility is that the sockets were for a wooden platform, allowing the funeral procession to pass over the granite plugs, which might have rested on the floor.

MASSIVE SECURITY

Between the Grand Gallery and the burial chamber there is an antechamber, with three slots carved in its walls. Each slot is 3 ft (91 cm) high and 21 in (54 cm) wide. These held granite portcullis slabs, which were probably lowered by ropes to seal the burial chamber after the funeral. Khufu had gone to unusual lengths to make his burial chamber a safe place—just as the chambers and passages created here were the most complex ever built within an Egyptian pyramid.

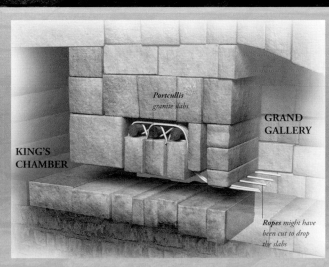

Portcullis granite slabs

KING'S CHAMBER

GRAND GALLERY

Ropes might have been cut to drop the slabs

CROSS-SECTION THROUGH THE ANTECHAMBER

corbeling Covering an opening by positioning each block overhanging the layer below to make the ceiling stronger.

antechamber A small room that is an entrance to the main room beyond—in this case, to the king's burial chamber.

portcullis A sliding slab or gate, lowered to seal an entrance.

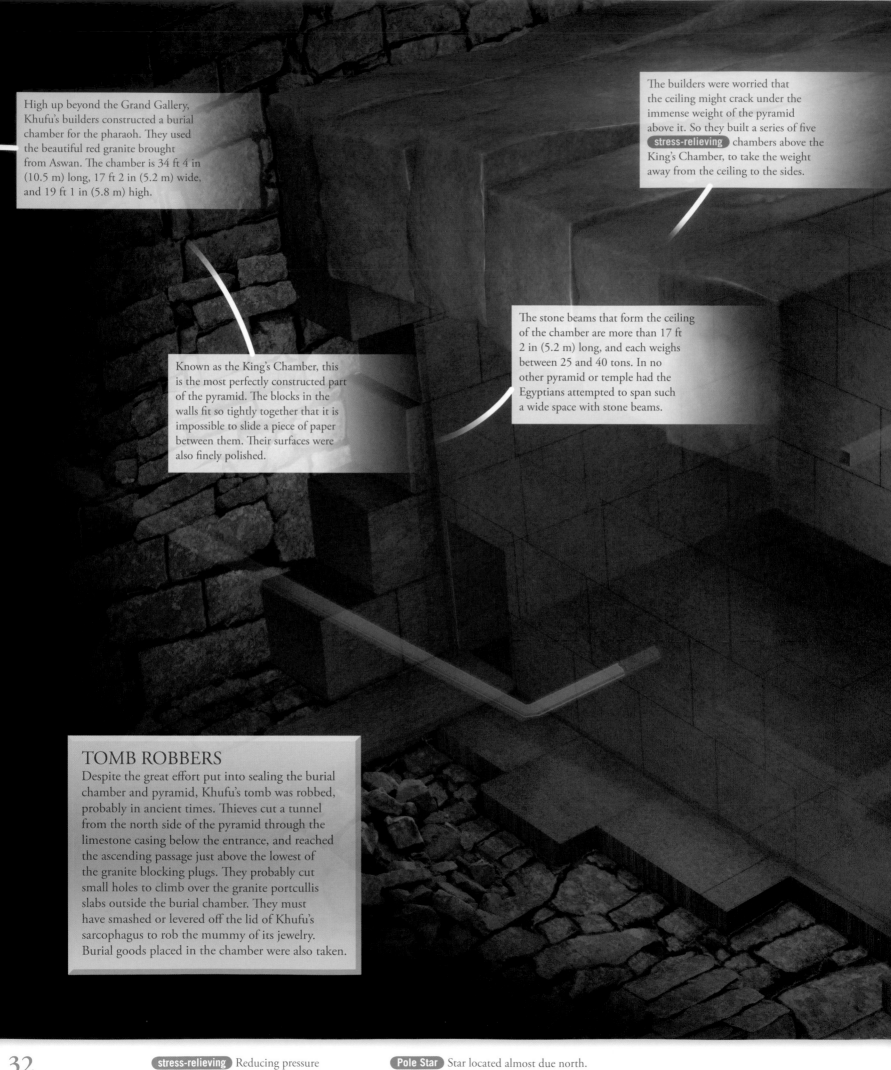

High up beyond the Grand Gallery, Khufu's builders constructed a burial chamber for the pharaoh. They used the beautiful red granite brought from Aswan. The chamber is 34 ft 4 in (10.5 m) long, 17 ft 2 in (5.2 m) wide, and 19 ft 1 in (5.8 m) high.

The builders were worried that the ceiling might crack under the immense weight of the pyramid above it. So they built a series of five **stress-relieving** chambers above the King's Chamber, to take the weight away from the ceiling to the sides.

Known as the King's Chamber, this is the most perfectly constructed part of the pyramid. The blocks in the walls fit so tightly together that it is impossible to slide a piece of paper between them. Their surfaces were also finely polished.

The stone beams that form the ceiling of the chamber are more than 17 ft 2 in (5.2 m) long, and each weighs between 25 and 40 tons. In no other pyramid or temple had the Egyptians attempted to span such a wide space with stone beams.

TOMB ROBBERS

Despite the great effort put into sealing the burial chamber and pyramid, Khufu's tomb was robbed, probably in ancient times. Thieves cut a tunnel from the north side of the pyramid through the limestone casing below the entrance, and reached the ascending passage just above the lowest of the granite blocking plugs. They probably cut small holes to climb over the granite portcullis slabs outside the burial chamber. They must have smashed or levered off the lid of Khufu's sarcophagus to rob the mummy of its jewelry. Burial goods placed in the chamber were also taken.

stress-relieving Reducing pressure or weight.

Pole Star Star located almost due north. The ancient Pole Star was Alpha Draconis, not the Pole Star we have today (Polaris).

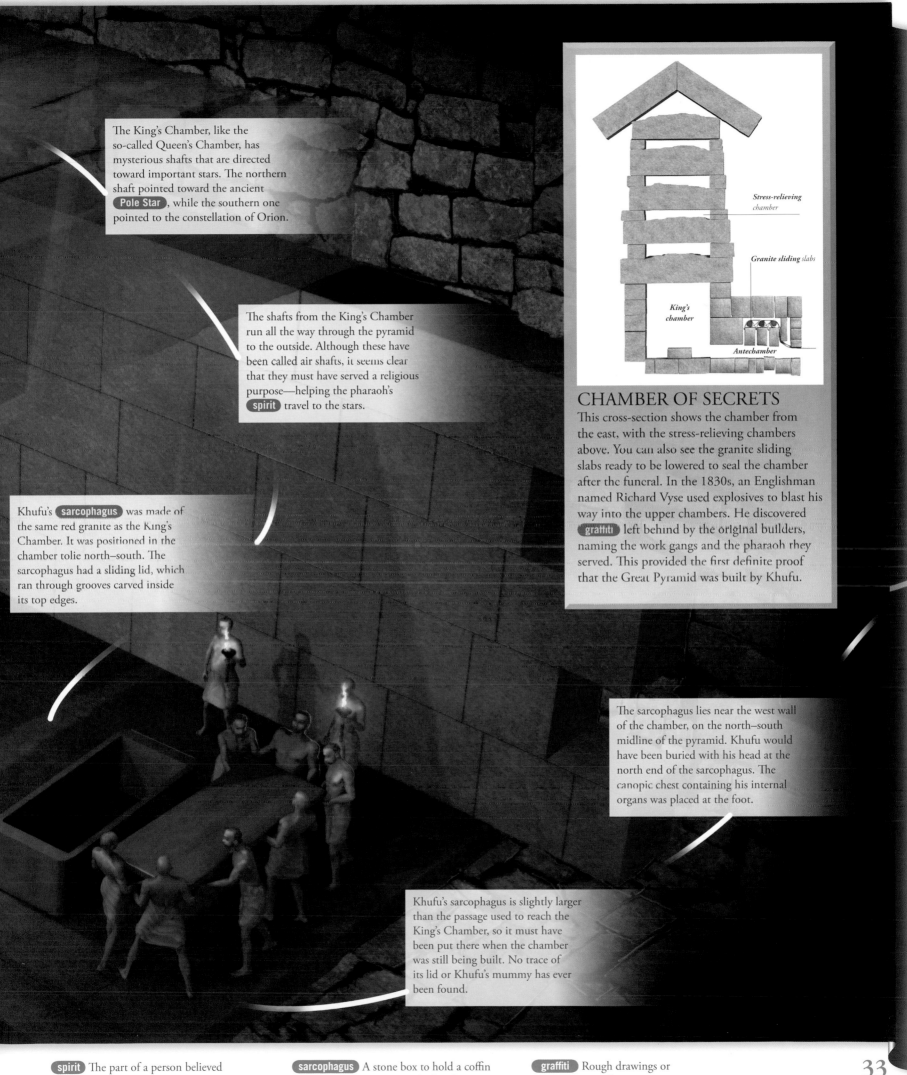

The King's Chamber, like the so-called Queen's Chamber, has mysterious shafts that are directed toward important stars. The northern shaft pointed toward the ancient **Pole Star**, while the southern one pointed to the constellation of Orion.

The shafts from the King's Chamber run all the way through the pyramid to the outside. Although these have been called air shafts, it seems clear that they must have served a religious purpose—helping the pharaoh's **spirit** travel to the stars.

Khufu's **sarcophagus** was made of the same red granite as the King's Chamber. It was positioned in the chamber tolie north–south. The sarcophagus had a sliding lid, which ran through grooves carved inside its top edges.

Stress-relieving chamber

Granite sliding slabs

King's chamber

Antechamber

CHAMBER OF SECRETS

This cross-section shows the chamber from the east, with the stress-relieving chambers above. You can also see the granite sliding slabs ready to be lowered to seal the chamber after the funeral. In the 1830s, an Englishman named Richard Vyse used explosives to blast his way into the upper chambers. He discovered **graffiti** left behind by the original builders, naming the work gangs and the pharaoh they served. This provided the first definite proof that the Great Pyramid was built by Khufu.

The sarcophagus lies near the west wall of the chamber, on the north–south midline of the pyramid. Khufu would have been buried with his head at the north end of the sarcophagus. The canopic chest containing his internal organs was placed at the foot.

Khufu's sarcophagus is slightly larger than the passage used to reach the King's Chamber, so it must have been put there when the chamber was still being built. No trace of its lid or Khufu's mummy has ever been found.

spirit The part of a person believed to go on living after death.

sarcophagus A stone box to hold a coffin and body. Sometimes inscribed with texts to help the deceased on their way to the next life.

graffiti Rough drawings or writings on a wall.

In Egypt you can sometimes see the sun's rays shining down through a break in the clouds at a similar angle to the slope of the pyramid. This suggests that, like the *ben-ben* stone, the complete pyramid was meant to be a model of the sun's rays.

Although the Great Pyramid's capstone has never been found, archaeologists have recently discovered a capstone from a small pyramid that Khufu also built at Giza. This was carved with a **convex** base, so that it would fit snugly onto **concave** stones beneath it.

Far above the burial chamber, the pyramid ends in a perfect point. The Egyptian name for the **capstone** at the top was *ben-benet*, after the *ben-ben*. This sacred stone in the temple of Re at Heliopolis represented the sun's life-giving rays. The pyramid itself was probably a copy of the ben-ben stone.

Like the small pyramid's capstone, the Great Pyramid's was probably made from plain white Turah limestone. Later capstones on other pyramids were carved from hard stones such as black granite. They were highly polished and decorated with religious **inscriptions** asking for help in the afterlife.

SETTING THE CAPSTONE

At the top of the pyramid, there was no longer enough space for the wide ramp used at the lower levels. There are many different theories to explain how the capstone was set. Egyptologist Dieter Arnold has suggested that a small stone stairway was built on one side of the pyramid. The workers brought the capstone up the stairway, perhaps on a wooden frame. They then levered it into place. There may also have been a small wooden platform for them to stand on as they maneuvered the stone into place.

capstone The top stone of the pyramid, which formed its point.

convex With a side that curves outward, like the outside of a bowl.

concave With a hollow side, like the inside of a bowl.

The capstone belonged at the top of the pyramid, nearly 490 ft (150 m) up, so it made a longer and more dangerous journey than any other stone. It was hauled all that way by hand. For the first part of its journey up the pyramid, it was probably dragged up the ramp on a slatted sledge.

For the last part of the journey, workers may have levered the capstone up to the top of the pyramid. Or perhaps they carried the capstone on a wooden frame. Either way, it would have been hard work, because the space the workers had to move in was very restricted so high up.

CELEBRATING THE SETTING OF THE CAPSTONE

The setting of the capstone was reported to the pharaoh, and offerings were made to the gods. **Reliefs** on the walls of the causeway at Abusir show scenes of dancers and wrestlers, along with officials and courtiers bowing toward the pyramid, and architects holding papyrus rolls, which may have held the plans for the pyramid itself. The relief shown here is from a later image of dancers and musicians with rattles and tambourines.

When the capstone was in place, the main building phase of the pyramid was finished. This was an important moment, so it was probably marked with great celebrations and religious ceremonies. However, the pyramid was not yet finished—there was still a lot more work to be done.

---

inscriptions Written or engraved form of words, in this case hieroglyphs.

reliefs Pictures carved onto flat stone surfaces in two dimensions.

SMOOTHING THE STONES

The pyramid built by Khufu's grandson, Menkaura, was left unfinished, perhaps because the pharaoh died before the end of construction. On its lower level today, it still has rough, undressed casing stones. This is good evidence that the pyramid was dressed from the top down. Where blocks have fallen away, the lines guiding the stonecutters can be seen on the sides of the casing stones. Since this method was used by Khufu's grandson, it may have been used by Khufu's builders as well.

As they worked their way down, the men might have stood on the projecting casing stones below them. They could also have used simple scaffolding made from light poles tied together with plant rope, as shown in Egyptian wall paintings.

Once the capstone was in place and celebrations finished, the stonecutters could begin to **dress** the casing stones. Workers also began to take down the enormous ramp they had used to bring the stone blocks and other materials up the pyramid.

The stonecutters were extremely skilled, working accurately to give each block a flat surface. When they finished, a different team of workers polished the blocks' surfaces by rubbing them with stones. This smoothed away the chisel marks, and made the stones gleam.

To cut away the stone sticking out from the angle of the pyramid's face, the stonecutters used small copper-bladed chisels. They were guided by the shape of the finished stones above, and by lines marked on the sides of the casing stones.

dress To cut back the rough parts of a stone to make it smooth and even.

debris A mass of unwanted material, such as rock pieces.

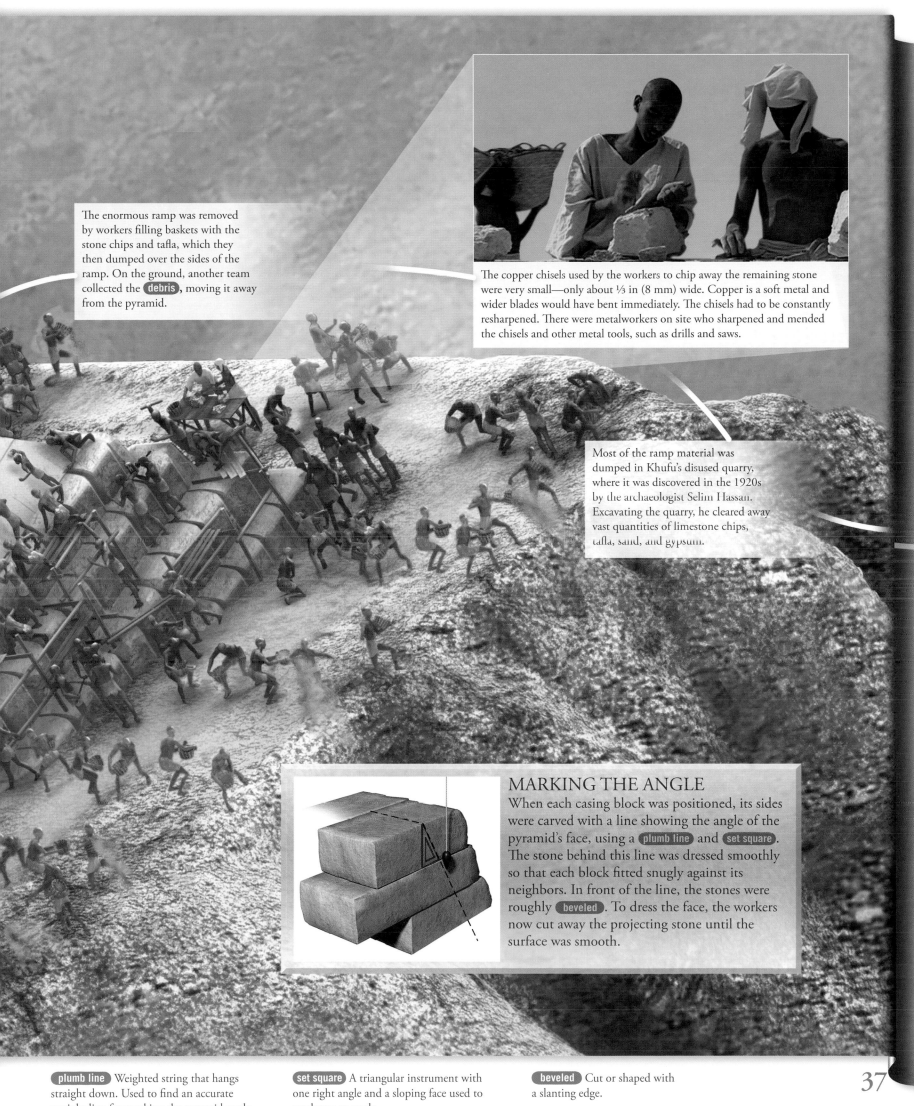

The enormous ramp was removed by workers filling baskets with the stone chips and tafla, which they then dumped over the sides of the ramp. On the ground, another team collected the debris, moving it away from the pyramid.

The copper chisels used by the workers to chip away the remaining stone were very small—only about ⅓ in (8 mm) wide. Copper is a soft metal and wider blades would have bent immediately. The chisels had to be constantly resharpened. There were metalworkers on site who sharpened and mended the chisels and other metal tools, such as drills and saws.

Most of the ramp material was dumped in Khufu's disused quarry, where it was discovered in the 1920s by the archaeologist Selim Hassan. Excavating the quarry, he cleared away vast quantities of limestone chips, tafla, sand, and gypsum.

MARKING THE ANGLE

When each casing block was positioned, its sides were carved with a line showing the angle of the pyramid's face, using a plumb line and set square. The stone behind this line was dressed smoothly so that each block fitted snugly against its neighbors. In front of the line, the stones were roughly beveled. To dress the face, the workers now cut away the projecting stone until the surface was smooth.

plumb line Weighted string that hangs straight down. Used to find an accurate upright line for marking the pyramid angle.

set square A triangular instrument with one right angle and a sloping face used to mark out an angle.

beveled Cut or shaped with a slanting edge.

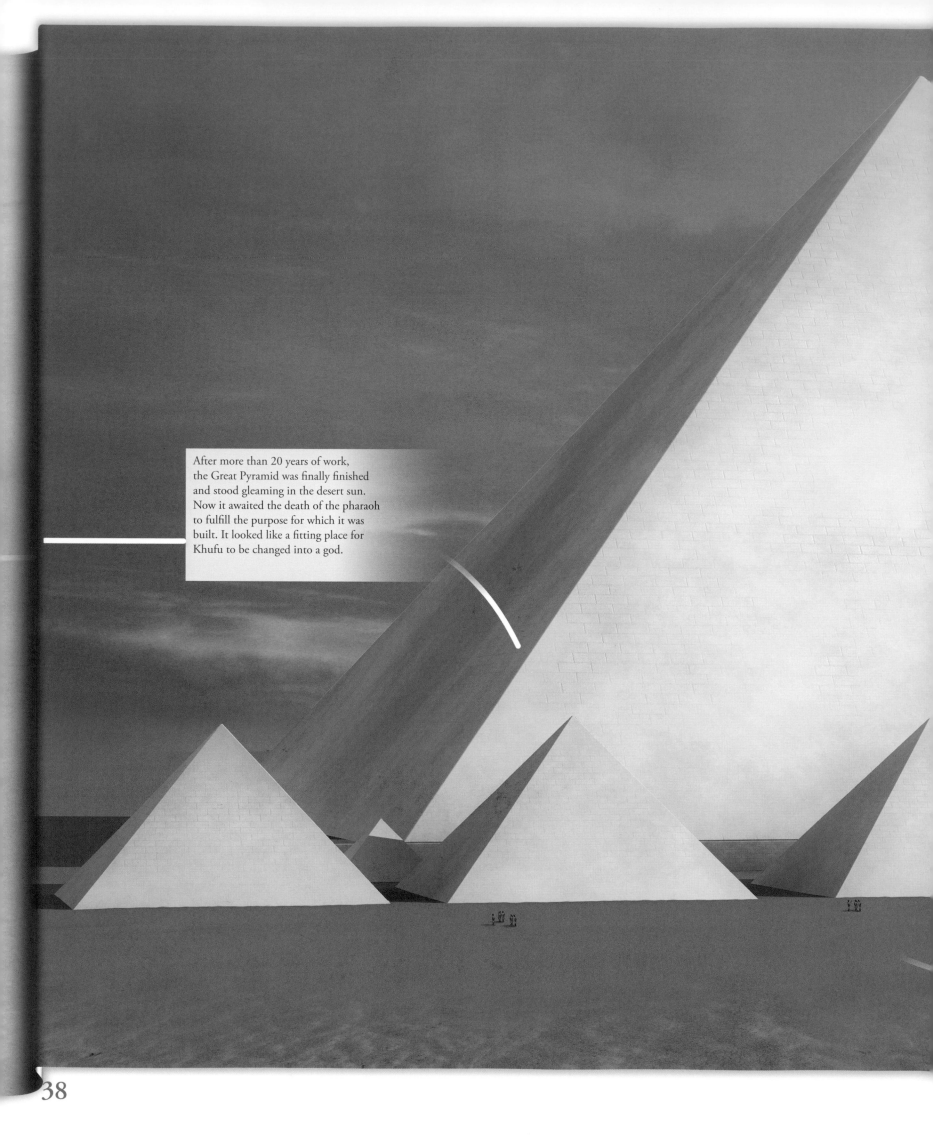

After more than 20 years of work, the Great Pyramid was finally finished and stood gleaming in the desert sun. Now it awaited the death of the pharaoh to fulfill the purpose for which it was built. It looked like a fitting place for Khufu to be changed into a god.

Although pharaohs would continue to build pyramids for more than a thousand years, none would ever match the size of the Great Pyramid. The ancient Greeks would later celebrate it as the greatest of the Seven Wonders of the World.

Thousands of Egyptians had helped to build Khufu's pyramid. Although the work had now come to an end, this was just a temporary pause. Soon there would be a new pharaoh, who would need his own pyramid, and so the hard work would start all over again.

Groups of wailing women mourned a pharaoh's death at his funeral, which was a time of great sorrow. This wall painting is inside a tomb dating from around 1370 BC.

broken, and this connection had to be restored. It was remade through rituals that placed Khufu in heaven and transferred his power to his son, Radjedef, the new pharaoh. The pyramid was the place where Khufu was changed into Osiris, and safely established in heaven.

> "He is on his way to heaven, on the wind. He is not hindered; there is no one by whom he is hindered."

Pyramid texts: Utterance 258, 2350–2150 BC

Pyramid texts
The burial chambers of later pyramids have magic spells written on the walls, designed to help the pharaoh change into Osiris and get to heaven. These spells, known as pyramid texts, take the form of hundreds of utterances, or sayings. There are none in Khufu's burial chamber, but they were probably spoken at his funeral by Radjedef or a priest.

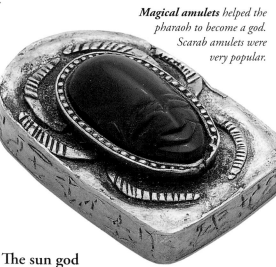

Magical amulets helped the pharaoh to become a god. Scarab amulets were very popular.

EXPLORING THE PAST

THE PHARAOH DIES

FUNERAL FOR A GOD

The death of a pharaoh, such as Khufu, was the most important event that could take place in ancient Egypt. For the pharaoh was no ordinary king. On Earth he was seen as the human form of the falcon-headed sky god, Horus. After death, he changed into Osiris, king of the dead and the father of Horus, and the new pharaoh replaced him on Earth as Horus.

Vital link
The living pharaoh provided a link between life on Earth and the gods, who made sure that all existence continued. It was thanks to the pharaoh that the sun rose every morning and the Nile River flooded at the right time so that crops could be grown. When Khufu died, the link between humanity and the gods was temporarily

The sun god
During Khufu's reign, the sun god Re became the most important Egyptian god. The pharaoh was now linked with Re as well as Osiris. So, unlike Djoser's Step Pyramid complex, which faced toward stars in the north, Khufu's pyramid complex was built facing east, toward the rising sun.

"Osiris dawns—pure, mighty, high, lord of truth."

Pyramid texts: Utterance 577, 2350–2150 BC

Sailing through the heavens

The Egyptians believed that Re traveled across the sky in a boat. At sunset, he passed below the western desert to the underworld. He then sailed back beneath the Earth, to reemerge at sunrise on the eastern horizon. This was the place where Re was reborn each morning. It was also where the dead pharaoh, riding in the boat of Re, first emerged as a god. This is why Khufu's pyramid was called *Akhet Khufu*, which means "the Horizon of Khufu."

Spirit forms

Ancient Egyptian ideas about life and death were complex. Everyone was thought to be made of

Ancient Egyptians thought of all journeys as being made by water. Just as Re crossed the sky in a boat, coffins were often taken to tombs on a boat resting on a sledge.

several parts, which all had to be protected after death. First, there was the physical body, which was preserved as a mummy—a perfect new body to last forever. There were also two spirit forms—the *ka* and the *ba*. The *ka* was the life force, which needed food to survive. A pharaoh's *ka* could enter his statues and receive food offerings on his behalf. The *ba* represented his ability to move around. So Khufu's *ba* could move between his mummy, high up in his pyramid, down to his temples to visit the *ka* statues, or travel up toward the stars. At the moment of death, the *ka*, *ba*, and body separated. They were brought back together during the funeral rituals. The *ka* and the *ba* now united as a third spirit form—the *akh*, meaning "shining light."

Funeral ceremonies

The central act performed by Radjedef at his father's funeral was called "the Opening of the Mouth." Playing the role of Horus, he brought his father back to life by magic. While reciting spells, he touched various parts of Khufu's mummy or *ka* statue with special tools, magically restoring all his father's bodily functions. Now Khufu could eat, breathe, and see again. He was ready to begin his new life in the next world.

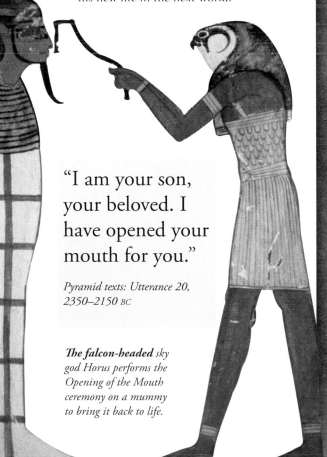

"I am your son, your beloved. I have opened your mouth for you."

Pyramid texts: Utterance 20, 2350–2150 BC

The falcon-headed sky god Horus performs the Opening of the Mouth ceremony on a mummy to bring it back to life.

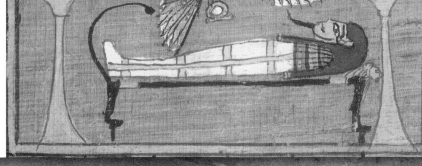

The ba spirit was pictured as a human-headed bird. In this papyrus painting, it hovers in midair over its mummy.

JOURNEY TO THE AFTERLIFE

When the pharaoh died, the Egyptians believed that he would travel up to the sky to join the gods. What we know of this journey comes from writings known as pyramid texts. These were written on the walls of burial chambers in later pyramids. They helped the pharaoh reach the sky. The pharaoh's journey is described in many different ways, to make him more likely to succeed. He leaps up into the sky as a grasshopper, is helped by winds and storms, or flies there as a falcon or goose. The Egyptians used hieroglyphs to record these texts.

To reach the new life, the pharaoh might pass through a pair of doors, at the point on the eastern horizon where the sun rose each day. The Egyptians thought this was where new life began. The pyramid texts declare, "The double doors of the horizon are opened!"

To reach the afterlife, the pharaoh traveled through the sky. Texts say that he rode in the beautiful boat of the sun god, Re, shown here as a hawk crowned with a sun disk. Images of the journey appear on wall friezes in later tombs.

Riding in the front of Re's boat is a heron, which lives on the river banks. Called the benu bird, this heron was sacred to Re and also linked with Osiris. This benu bird is wearing Osiris's feathered crown.

hieroglyphs Pictures and symbols used by Egyptians to represent words, syllables, or sounds as a system of writing.

The pyramid texts include many different beliefs, developed over hundreds of years. So the pharaoh is described as Osiris, but is also welcomed by the god in the afterlife. Here a man is being led to Osiris by Anubis, god of mummification.

On his journey to the afterlife, the pharaoh was reborn as Osiris, king of the dead. Osiris is shown wearing white mummy wrappings and holding a **crook** and a **flail**, both royal emblems. He has a special crown with feathers, called an atef, and a false beard, another mark of royalty.

While the dead pharaoh became Osiris, his son on earth replaced him as the new form of Horus, the falcon-headed sky god. Horus's two eyes are staring out on either side of his father Osiris. These represented the sun and the moon. While Osiris ruled over the dead, Horus ruled over the living.

crook A stick with a hook at one end, used by shepherds to guide sheep. Carried as a symbol of Egyptian kings.

flail An Egyptian royal symbol, which may have been a whip or a whisk for driving away flies.

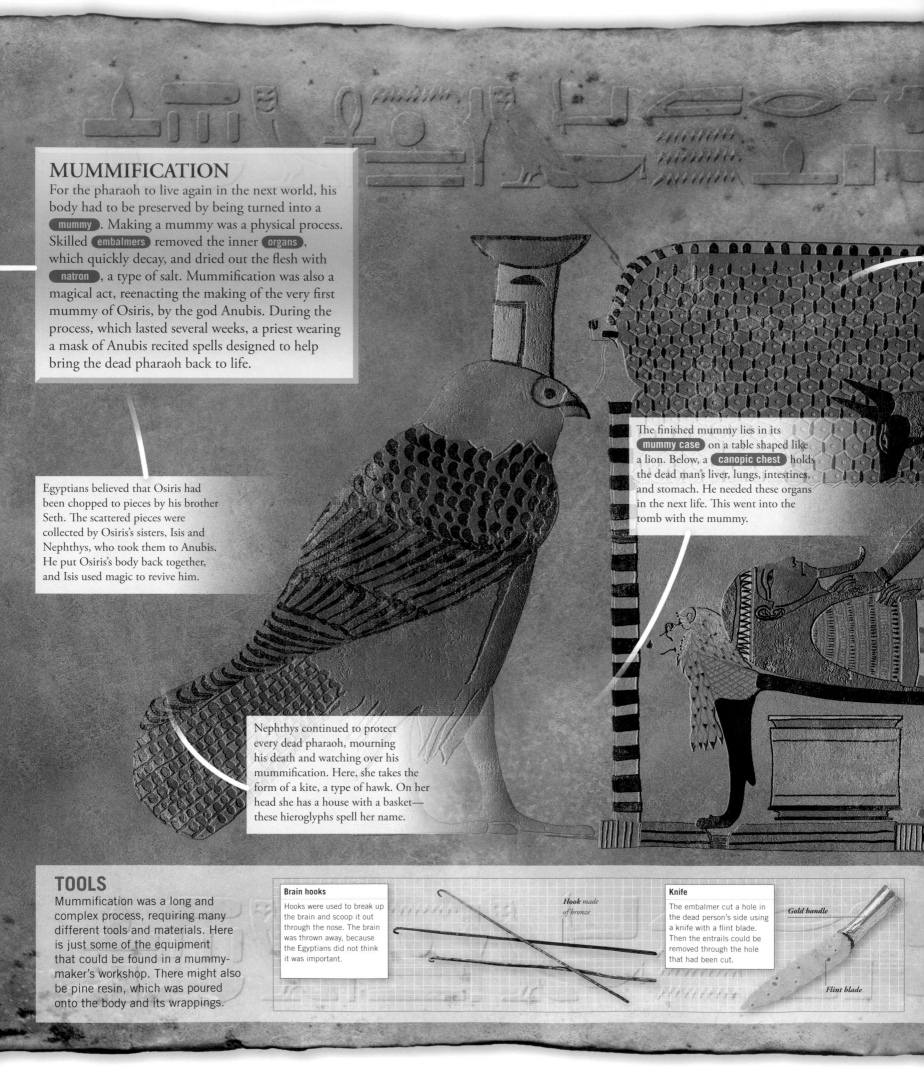

MUMMIFICATION

For the pharaoh to live again in the next world, his body had to be preserved by being turned into a mummy . Making a mummy was a physical process. Skilled embalmers removed the inner organs , which quickly decay, and dried out the flesh with natron , a type of salt. Mummification was also a magical act, reenacting the making of the very first mummy of Osiris, by the god Anubis. During the process, which lasted several weeks, a priest wearing a mask of Anubis recited spells designed to help bring the dead pharaoh back to life.

Egyptians believed that Osiris had been chopped to pieces by his brother Seth. The scattered pieces were collected by Osiris's sisters, Isis and Nephthys, who took them to Anubis. He put Osiris's body back together, and Isis used magic to revive him.

The finished mummy lies in its mummy case on a table shaped like a lion. Below, a canopic chest holds the dead man's liver, lungs, intestines, and stomach. He needed these organs in the next life. This went into the tomb with the mummy.

Nephthys continued to protect every dead pharaoh, mourning his death and watching over his mummification. Here, she takes the form of a kite, a type of hawk. On her head she has a house with a basket— these hieroglyphs spell her name.

TOOLS

Mummification was a long and complex process, requiring many different tools and materials. Here is just some of the equipment that could be found in a mummy-maker's workshop. There might also be pine resin, which was poured onto the body and its wrappings.

Brain hooks
Hooks were used to break up the brain and scoop it out through the nose. The brain was thrown away, because the Egyptians did not think it was important.

Hook made of bronze

Knife
The embalmer cut a hole in the dead person's side using a knife with a flint blade. Then the entrails could be removed through the hole that had been cut.

Gold handle

Flint blade

mummy A dead body that has been preserved from decay, either naturally or (as in ancient Egypt) artificially.

embalmers People who artificially preserve a dead body, using salts, perfumes, ointments, and (nowadays) chemicals.

organs Parts of the body, such as the lungs or the stomach, that have a particular function of their own.

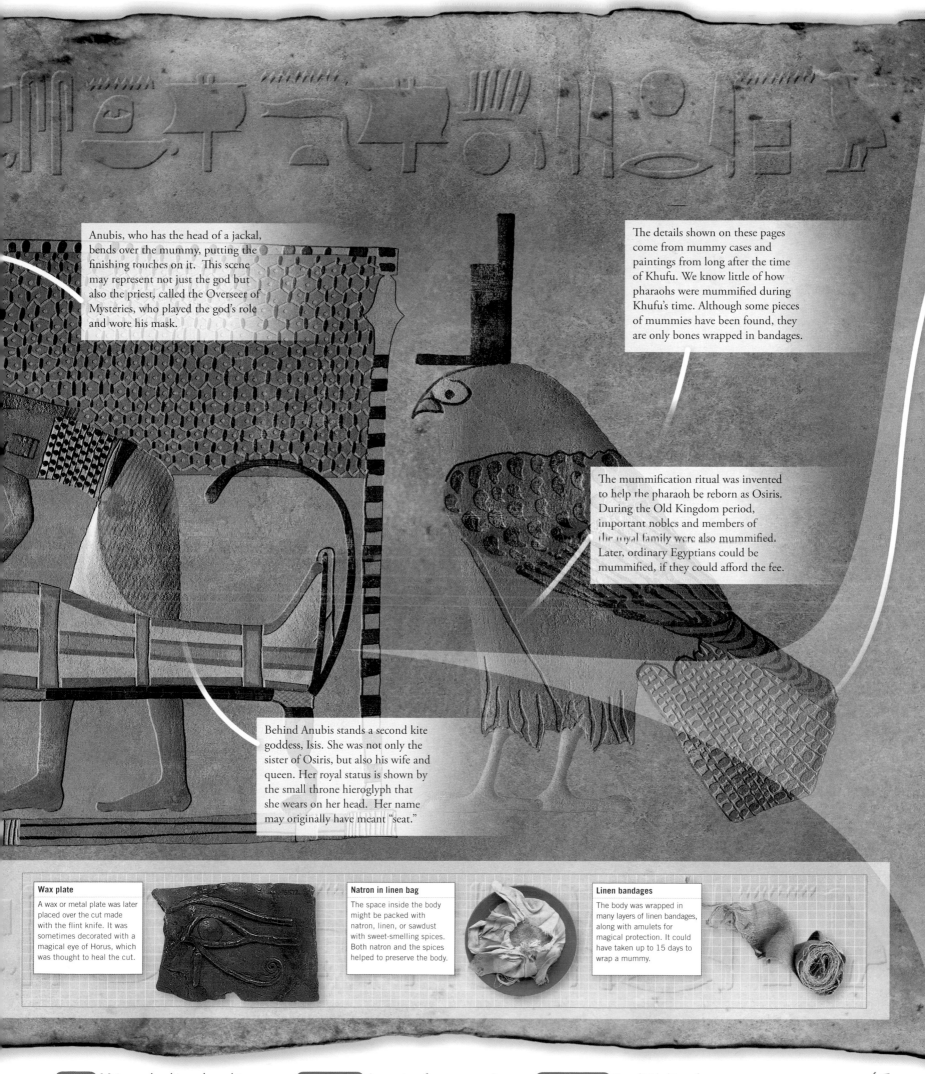

Anubis, who has the head of a jackal, bends over the mummy, putting the finishing touches on it. This scene may represent not just the god but also the priest, called the Overseer of Mysteries, who played the god's role and wore his mask.

The details shown on these pages come from mummy cases and paintings from long after the time of Khufu. We know little of how pharaohs were mummified during Khufu's time. Although some pieces of mummies have been found, they are only bones wrapped in bandages.

The mummification ritual was invented to help the pharaoh be reborn as Osiris. During the Old Kingdom period, important nobles and members of the royal family were also mummified. Later, ordinary Egyptians could be mummified, if they could afford the fee.

Behind Anubis stands a second kite goddess, Isis. She was not only the sister of Osiris, but also his wife and queen. Her royal status is shown by the small throne hieroglyph that she wears on her head. Her name may originally have meant "seat."

Wax plate
A wax or metal plate was later placed over the cut made with the flint knife. It was sometimes decorated with a magical eye of Horus, which was thought to heal the cut.

Natron in linen bag
The space inside the body might be packed with natron, linen, or sawdust with sweet-smelling spices. Both natron and the spices helped to preserve the body.

Linen bandages
The body was wrapped in many layers of linen bandages, along with amulets for magical protection. It could have taken up to 15 days to wrap a mummy.

natron Moisture-absorbing salt used in ancient Egypt to dry out a corpse. The salt comes from dried lake beds.

mummy case A container for a mummy. In Khufu's time, these were plain boxes. Later they resembled mummies.

canopic chest Box divided into four sections for storing embalmed organs. Later, the organs were stored in canopic jars.

A TRANSPARENT 3-D MUMMY

In the past, the only way to examine a mummy was to unwrap it, usually destroying it in the process. Now Egyptologists can use **CT scans** to look inside a mummy's wrappings without even opening the wooden mummy case. The scans help us to understand the mummification process. This is the mummy of a man who died around 800 BC. His teeth reveal that he was in his early forties. The writing on his mummy case says that he was a priest called Nesperennub, who served in the temple at Karnak.

The CT scans reveal a rough clay bowl behind the mummy's head. This was probably left here to catch the **resin** smeared over Nesperennub's skin. Perhaps the embalmers left the bowl in place for too long—when the resin dried hard, it glued the bowl to Nesperennub's head.

The mummy's eye sockets contain artificial eyes, probably made from stone or glass. Human eyes could not be preserved by mummification. Damage around the nose shows where the brain was pulled out by the embalmers, using metal hooks.

The mummy case has a portrait of Nesperennub, shown as a young man with a peaceful expression and a long, dark wig. This was an **idealized** portrait of Nesperennub, and probably bore little resemblance to the real man.

The mummy case is covered with magical symbols, including a **scarab** with beautifully painted wings that wrap around Nesperennub's upper body. The scarab represented rebirth, while the stretched-out wings are protective.

CT scans Computed tomography scans, a computerized X-ray procedure that produces detailed cross-sectional images of the body.

resin Sap from a tree that is often used in varnishes. When it dries, it can become hard and form a protective coating.

idealized Made perfect.

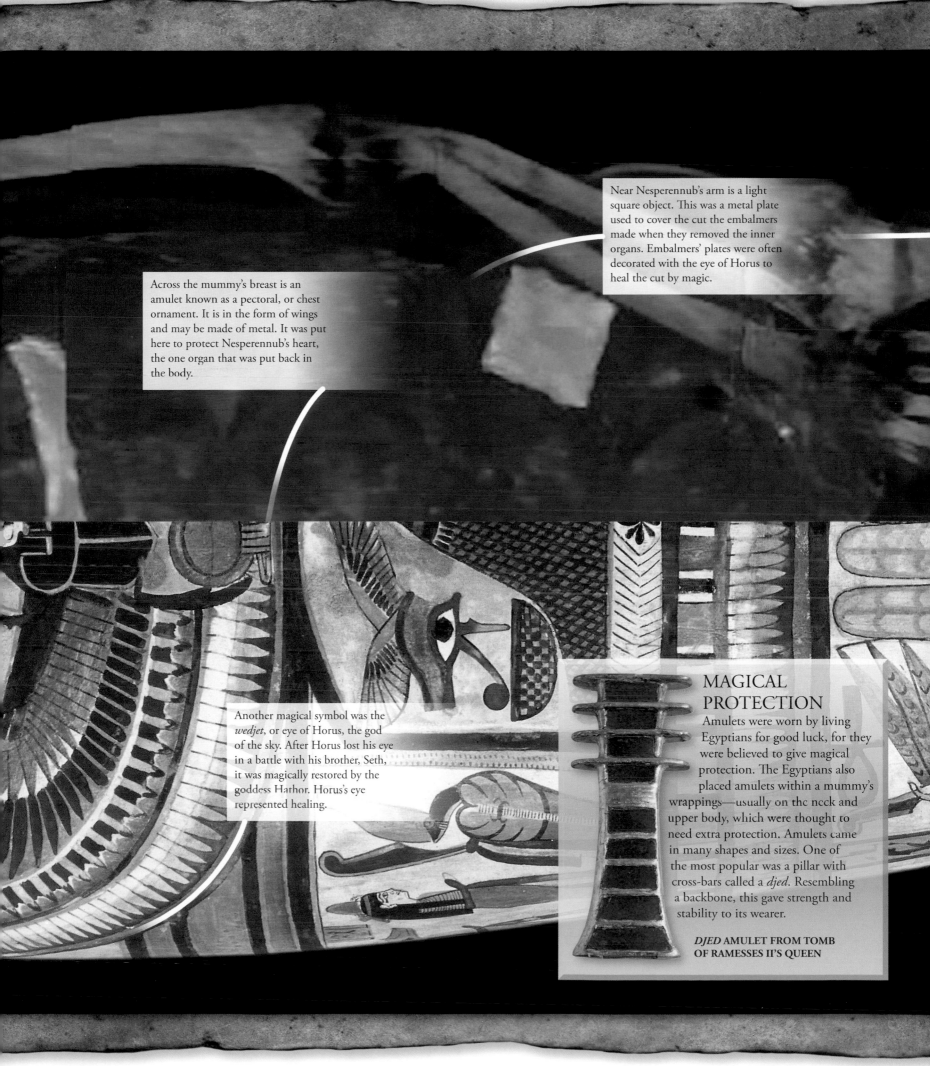

Near Nesperennub's arm is a light square object. This was a metal plate used to cover the cut the embalmers made when they removed the inner organs. Embalmers' plates were often decorated with the eye of Horus to heal the cut by magic.

Across the mummy's breast is an amulet known as a pectoral, or chest ornament. It is in the form of wings and may be made of metal. It was put here to protect Nesperennub's heart, the one organ that was put back in the body.

Another magical symbol was the *wedjet*, or eye of Horus, the god of the sky. After Horus lost his eye in a battle with his brother, Seth, it was magically restored by the goddess Hathor. Horus's eye represented healing.

MAGICAL PROTECTION

Amulets were worn by living Egyptians for good luck, for they were believed to give magical protection. The Egyptians also placed amulets within a mummy's wrappings—usually on the neck and upper body, which were thought to need extra protection. Amulets came in many shapes and sizes. One of the most popular was a pillar with cross-bars called a *djed*. Resembling a backbone, this gave strength and stability to its wearer.

DJED AMULET FROM TOMB OF RAMESSES II'S QUEEN

scarab An Egyptian dung-beetle, and also a gem carved to resemble one. The ancient Egyptians believed it brought good luck.

Picture credit: Visualisation of Nesperennub courtesy of Silicon Graphics Ltd/The British Museum

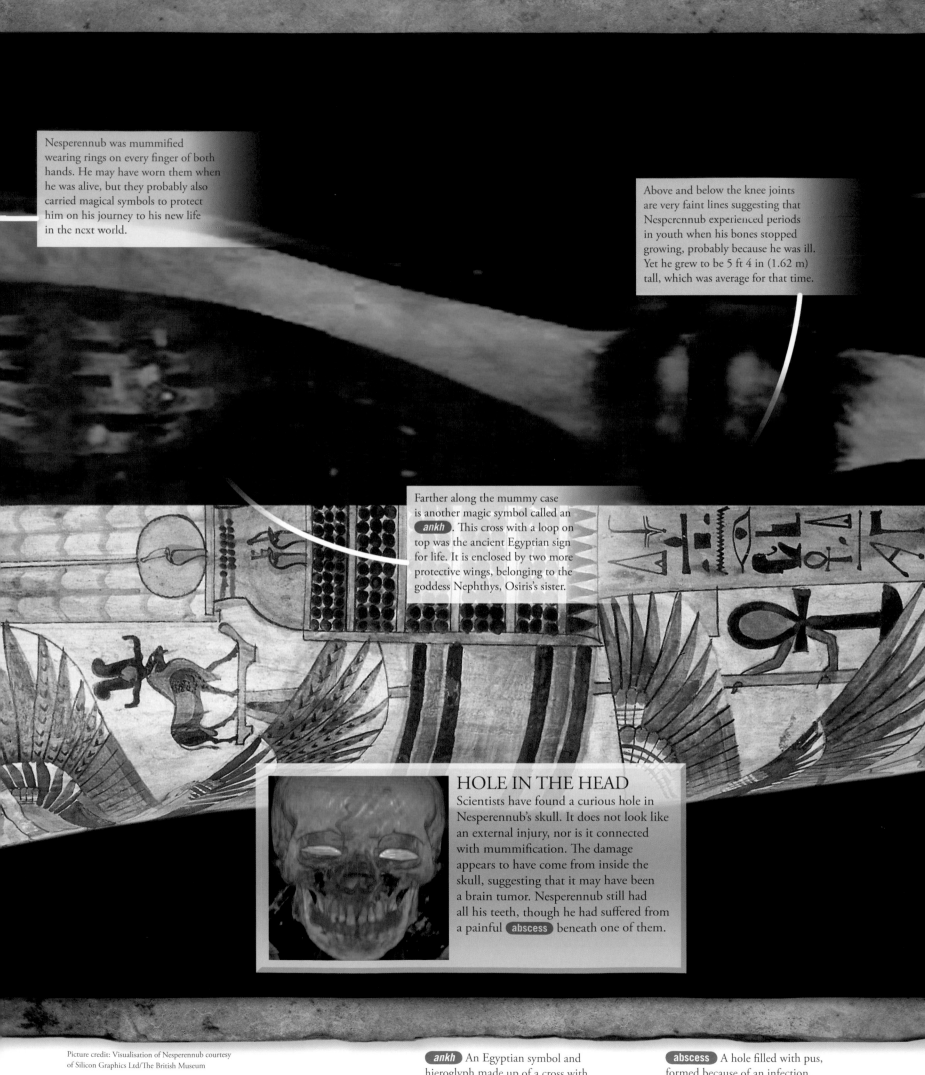

Nesperennub was mummified wearing rings on every finger of both hands. He may have worn them when he was alive, but they probably also carried magical symbols to protect him on his journey to his new life in the next world.

Above and below the knee joints are very faint lines suggesting that Nesperennub experienced periods in youth when his bones stopped growing, probably because he was ill. Yet he grew to be 5 ft 4 in (1.62 m) tall, which was average for that time.

Farther along the mummy case is another magic symbol called an **ankh**. This cross with a loop on top was the ancient Egyptian sign for life. It is enclosed by two more protective wings, belonging to the goddess Nephthys, Osiris's sister.

HOLE IN THE HEAD

Scientists have found a curious hole in Nesperennub's skull. It does not look like an external injury, nor is it connected with mummification. The damage appears to have come from inside the skull, suggesting that it may have been a brain tumor. Nesperennub still had all his teeth, though he had suffered from a painful **abscess** beneath one of them.

Picture credit: Visualisation of Nesperennub courtesy of Silicon Graphics Ltd/The British Museum

ankh An Egyptian symbol and hieroglyph made up of a cross with a loop on top.

abscess A hole filled with pus, formed because of an infection.

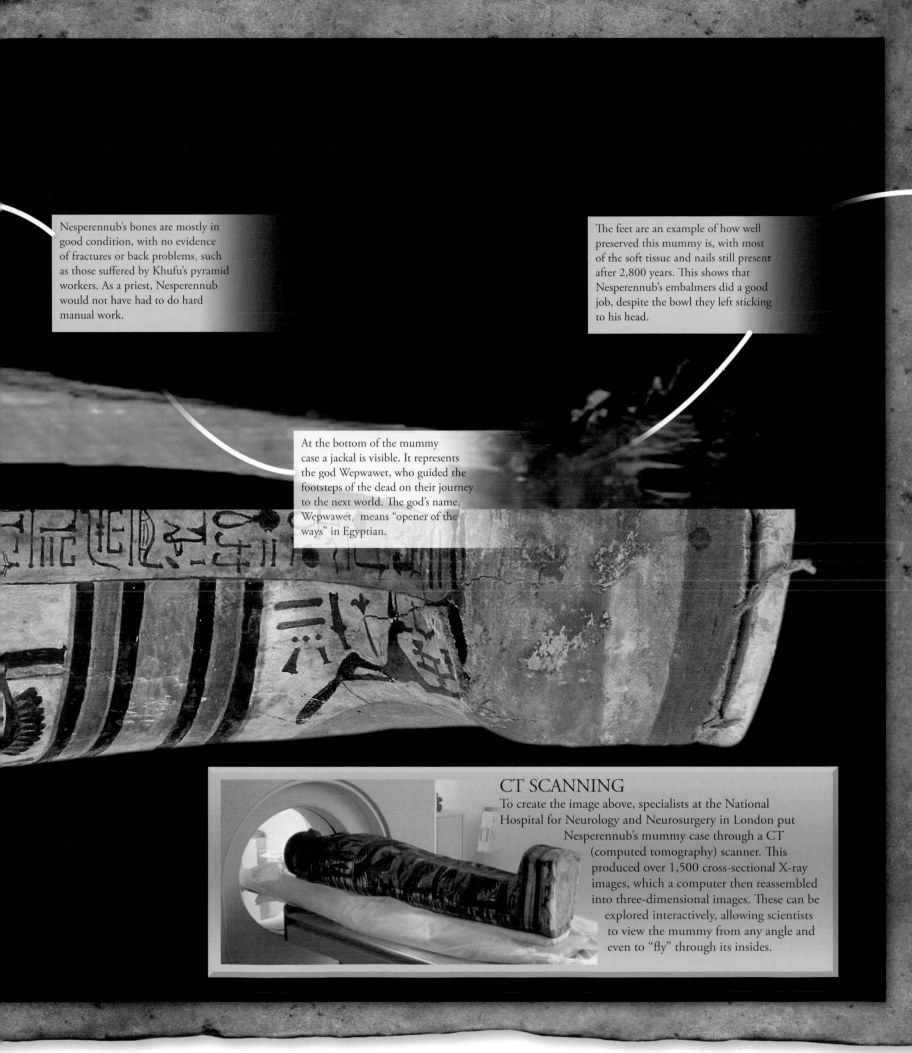

Nesperennub's bones are mostly in good condition, with no evidence of fractures or back problems, such as those suffered by Khufu's pyramid workers. As a priest, Nesperennub would not have had to do hard manual work.

The feet are an example of how well preserved this mummy is, with most of the soft tissue and nails still present after 2,800 years. This shows that Nesperennub's embalmers did a good job, despite the bowl they left sticking to his head.

At the bottom of the mummy case a jackal is visible. It represents the god Wepwawet, who guided the footsteps of the dead on their journey to the next world. The god's name, Wepwawet, means "opener of the ways" in Egyptian.

CT SCANNING

To create the image above, specialists at the National Hospital for Neurology and Neurosurgery in London put Nesperennub's mummy case through a CT (computed tomography) scanner. This produced over 1,500 cross-sectional X-ray images, which a computer then reassembled into three-dimensional images. These can be explored interactively, allowing scientists to view the mummy from any angle and even to "fly" through its insides.

TO THE PYRAMID

Once Khufu's mummy was ready, it was taken in a funeral procession to his pyramid, where it would be placed in the granite sarcophagus. The procession was overseen by Khufu's son, Radjedef, who would replace him as the new pharaoh on Earth. The procession probably began at the Nile and then moved up the long causeway toward the pyramid. The Egyptian name for a causeway meant "the place of the haul," and later images show the pharaoh's coffin being hauled on a sledge.

These men carry a chair and chests containing clothing and jewelry— just some of the supplies for the new house that Khufu would set up in the next world. In 1925, American archaeologist George Reisner found similar grave goods belonging to Khufu's mother, Hetepheres.

The procession included priests, who recited magic spells, and women playing the roles of Isis and Nephthys, the goddesses who mourned for Osiris. These servants carry jars of wine to be placed in the tomb.

Khufu's personal belongings were carried in the procession, because the Egyptians believed that he could take them with him to the afterlife. Two men carry a bed with a headrest, and a feather fan to keep the pharaoh cool in the afterlife.

causeway A raised or paved roadway. Egyptian causeways were enclosed by high walls, and sometimes covered by a roof.

grave goods Objects placed in a grave or tomb, for use in the next life—furniture, jewels, weapons, boats, even models of slaves.

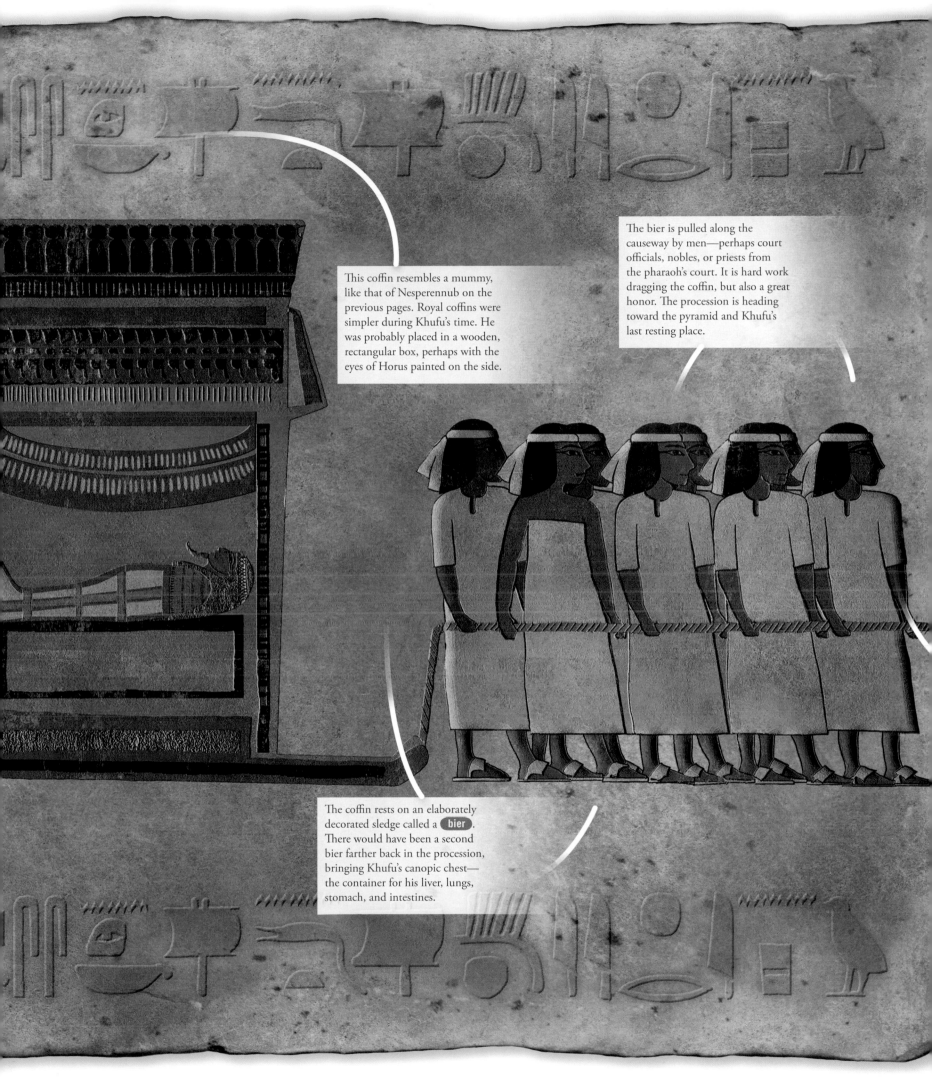

This coffin resembles a mummy, like that of Nesperennub on the previous pages. Royal coffins were simpler during Khufu's time. He was probably placed in a wooden, rectangular box, perhaps with the eyes of Horus painted on the side.

The bier is pulled along the causeway by men—perhaps court officials, nobles, or priests from the pharaoh's court. It is hard work dragging the coffin, but also a great honor. The procession is heading toward the pyramid and Khufu's last resting place.

The coffin rests on an elaborately decorated sledge called a **bier**. There would have been a second bier farther back in the procession, bringing Khufu's canopic chest— the container for his liver, lungs, stomach, and intestines.

bier A stand for a coffin before burial. This bier is a couch resting beneath a covering called a canopy.

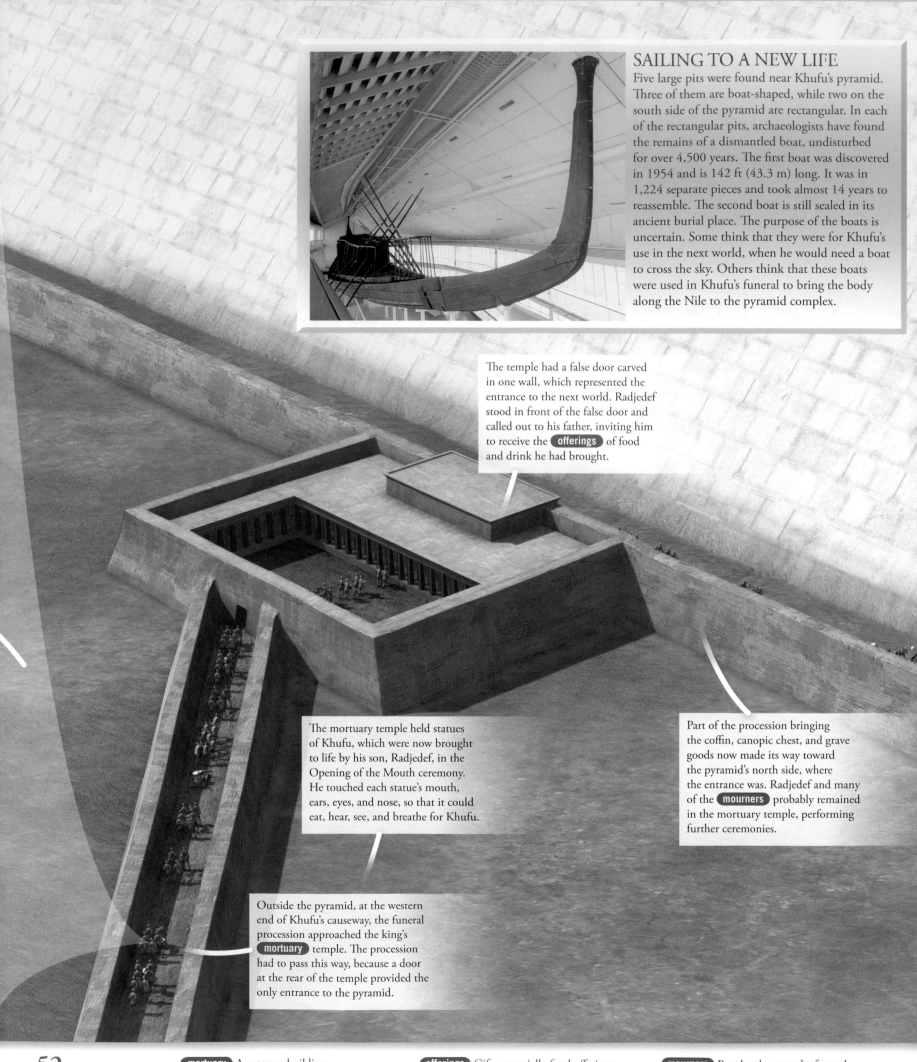

SAILING TO A NEW LIFE

Five large pits were found near Khufu's pyramid. Three of them are boat-shaped, while two on the south side of the pyramid are rectangular. In each of the rectangular pits, archaeologists have found the remains of a dismantled boat, undisturbed for over 4,500 years. The first boat was discovered in 1954 and is 142 ft (43.3 m) long. It was in 1,224 separate pieces and took almost 14 years to reassemble. The second boat is still sealed in its ancient burial place. The purpose of the boats is uncertain. Some think that they were for Khufu's use in the next world, when he would need a boat to cross the sky. Others think that these boats were used in Khufu's funeral to bring the body along the Nile to the pyramid complex.

The temple had a false door carved in one wall, which represented the entrance to the next world. Radjedef stood in front of the false door and called out to his father, inviting him to receive the **offerings** of food and drink he had brought.

The mortuary temple held statues of Khufu, which were now brought to life by his son, Radjedef, in the Opening of the Mouth ceremony. He touched each statue's mouth, ears, eyes, and nose, so that it could eat, hear, see, and breathe for Khufu.

Part of the procession bringing the coffin, canopic chest, and grave goods now made its way toward the pyramid's north side, where the entrance was. Radjedef and many of the **mourners** probably remained in the mortuary temple, performing further ceremonies.

Outside the pyramid, at the western end of Khufu's causeway, the funeral procession approached the king's **mortuary** temple. The procession had to pass this way, because a door at the rear of the temple provided the only entrance to the pyramid.

mortuary A room or building linked with death.

offerings Gifts, especially food offerings, given to the gods and dead pharaohs in their temples.

mourners People who attend a funeral. The pharaoh's mourners would include priests, family, and courtiers.

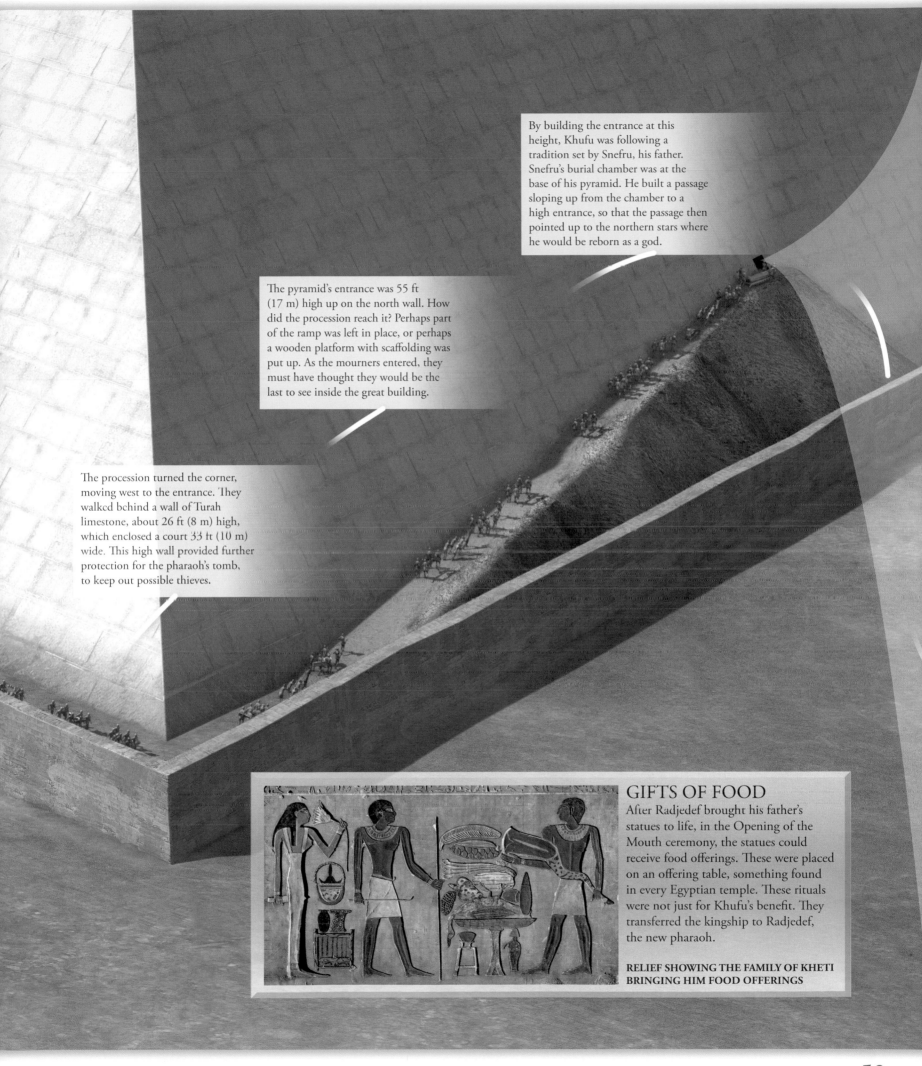

By building the entrance at this height, Khufu was following a tradition set by Snefru, his father. Snefru's burial chamber was at the base of his pyramid. He built a passage sloping up from the chamber to a high entrance, so that the passage then pointed up to the northern stars where he would be reborn as a god.

The pyramid's entrance was 55 ft (17 m) high up on the north wall. How did the procession reach it? Perhaps part of the ramp was left in place, or perhaps a wooden platform with scaffolding was put up. As the mourners entered, they must have thought they would be the last to see inside the great building.

The procession turned the corner, moving west to the entrance. They walked behind a wall of Turah limestone, about 26 ft (8 m) high, which enclosed a court 33 ft (10 m) wide. This high wall provided further protection for the pharaoh's tomb, to keep out possible thieves.

GIFTS OF FOOD

After Radjedef brought his father's statues to life, in the Opening of the Mouth ceremony, the statues could receive food offerings. These were placed on an offering table, something found in every Egyptian temple. These rituals were not just for Khufu's benefit. They transferred the kingship to Radjedef, the new pharaoh.

RELIEF SHOWING THE FAMILY OF KHETI BRINGING HIM FOOD OFFERINGS

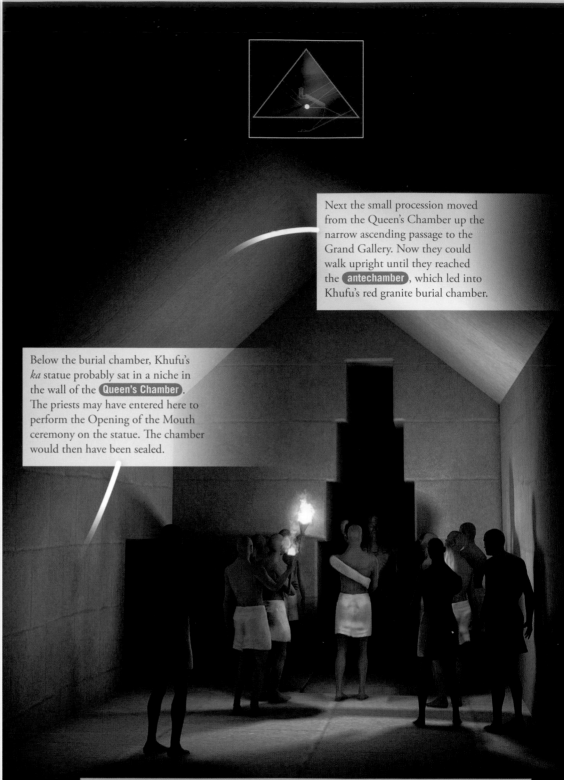

Next the small procession moved from the Queen's Chamber up the narrow ascending passage to the Grand Gallery. Now they could walk upright until they reached the **antechamber**, which led into Khufu's red granite burial chamber.

Below the burial chamber, Khufu's *ka* statue probably sat in a niche in the wall of the **Queen's Chamber**. The priests may have entered here to perform the Opening of the Mouth ceremony on the statue. The chamber would then have been sealed.

Inside the pyramid, the priests and their helpers dragged Khufu's wooden coffin up the cramped ascending passage toward the burial chamber. They carried flaming torches to light their way. Attendants brought up the offerings for Khufu.

THE *KA* STATUE

Khufu's *ka* statue has never been found. The evidence that it existed is the niche in the Queen's Chamber. Egyptians often built niches for statues, and *ka* statues of other pharaohs have been found in sealed chambers called **serdabs**. This is Djoser's *ka* statue, placed in a serdab beside his pyramid. Peepholes were carved in the serdab walls, angled upward, so that the *ka* could gaze up to the stars.

Queen's Chamber A room below the king's burial chamber. Once thought, mistakenly, to be the burial chamber for Khufu's queen.

antechamber A small room that is an entrance to the main room beyond—in this case, to Khufu's burial chamber.

The pharaoh's precious belongings, which he would need in the next world, were placed on the floor around the chamber. We can only guess what treasures they might have included— thieves stole them all.

Now the procession left the chamber. Most of the priests probably left the pyramid the way they had come in. A few men remained behind to seal the burial chamber by dropping the granite portcullis slabs in the antechamber.

The men then released the granite blocks stored in the Grand Gallery, which slid down, crashing on the bottom to seal the ascending passage. As the sound echoed around the Grand Gallery, the men inside were left to make their own way out.

The coffin was placed in the granite sarcophagus. Priests recited more spells to help the pharaoh be reborn as Osiris and unite with Re, the sun god. The sarcophagus was then sealed by sliding the heavy lid shut. But even that would not save Khufu from thieves.

The only way out was the deep and dark escape shaft. They had to climb 100 ft (30 m) down to the descending passage, which they used to leave the pyramid. The exit was sealed behind them and Khufu was alone in his resting place.

serdabs The name comes from an Arabic word meaning cellar. The Egyptian name was *per-twt* (statue house).

The pyramid was now complete. Called *Akhet Khufu* ("The Horizon of Khufu"), it was the center of a religious **complex**, with smaller pyramids and **mastaba** tombs. There were also two temples where Khufu was worshiped as a god.

To the east, south, and west, there were dozens of low mastaba tombs, where Khufu's high officials and relatives were buried. It was a great honor to be allowed to be buried near the pharaoh, sharing in the afterlife with him.

N

By the southeast corner of the pyramid stood a little **satellite** pyramid. It was usual to build such pyramids, though their purpose remains a mystery. One theory is that it was built for Khufu's *ka*, his life force.

complex An area made up of many structures linked together by a common purpose.

mastaba A long, low, rectangular tomb, named after the Arabic word for "bench."

satellite A small object, here a building, that is associated with a larger one.

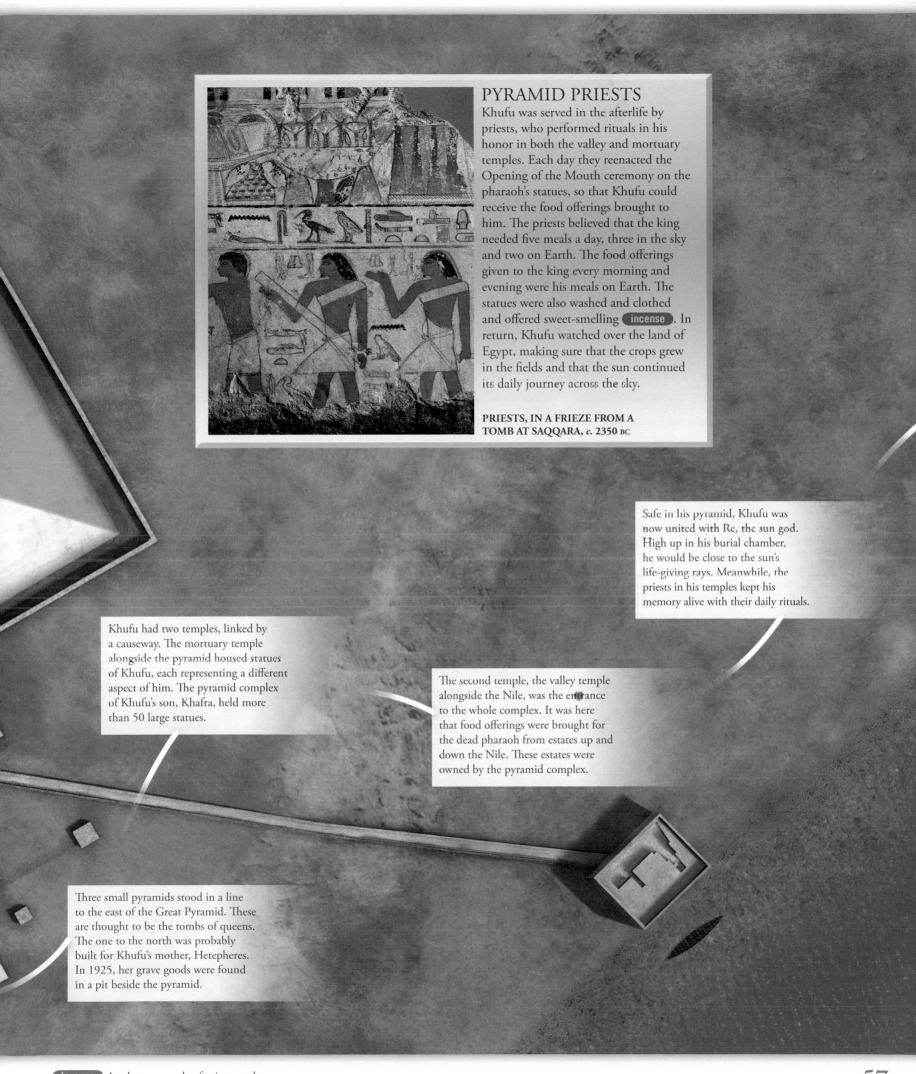

PYRAMID PRIESTS

Khufu was served in the afterlife by priests, who performed rituals in his honor in both the valley and mortuary temples. Each day they reenacted the Opening of the Mouth ceremony on the pharaoh's statues, so that Khufu could receive the food offerings brought to him. The priests believed that the king needed five meals a day, three in the sky and two on Earth. The food offerings given to the king every morning and evening were his meals on Earth. The statues were also washed and clothed and offered sweet-smelling incense. In return, Khufu watched over the land of Egypt, making sure that the crops grew in the fields and that the sun continued its daily journey across the sky.

PRIESTS, IN A FRIEZE FROM A TOMB AT SAQQARA, *c.* **2350** BC

Safe in his pyramid, Khufu was now united with Re, the sun god. High up in his burial chamber, he would be close to the sun's life-giving rays. Meanwhile, the priests in his temples kept his memory alive with their daily rituals.

Khufu had two temples, linked by a causeway. The mortuary temple alongside the pyramid housed statues of Khufu, each representing a different aspect of him. The pyramid complex of Khufu's son, Khafra, held more than 50 large statues.

The second temple, the valley temple alongside the Nile, was the entrance to the whole complex. It was here that food offerings were brought for the dead pharaoh from estates up and down the Nile. These estates were owned by the pyramid complex.

Three small pyramids stood in a line to the east of the Great Pyramid. These are thought to be the tombs of queens. The one to the north was probably built for Khufu's mother, Hetepheres. In 1925, her grave goods were found in a pit beside the pyramid.

incense A substance made of spices used to produce a fragrant smell when burned.

57

In this engraving, Napoleon Bonaparte examines the granite sarcophagus in the King's Chamber, questioning his Egyptian guides.

"One of the men narrowly escaped being crushed to pieces. A large block of stone… fell from the top while the man was digging."

Giovanni Belzoni, in Narrative of Operations and Recent Discoveries in Egypt and Nubia*, 1822, on the dangers of digging into Khafra's pyramid*

EXPLORING THE PAST

REDISCOVERY

THE PYRAMIDS' SECRETS ARE REVEALED

Despite all of Khufu's security measures, his pyramid was still robbed in ancient times, like every other Egyptian pyramid. The thieves may even have been workers who had helped to build the pyramid. They knew exactly where to tunnel in to find their way around the granite blocks sealing the ascending passage.

Exposed!

After the pyramid was broken into, it lay open to visitors and swarms of bats, which nested there for thousands of years. The finely polished outer casing stones were also stripped away. They were reused as construction materials, probably to build the new town of Cairo, founded in AD 969.

Crawling inside

In 1765, an Englishman named Nathaniel Davison made the first new discoveries at the Great Pyramid. He found an opening high up on the wall of the Grand Gallery. After crawling through layers of foul-smelling bat dung, with a handkerchief over his mouth to stop him from being sick, he came across the first relieving chamber, above the burial chamber. This is still known as Davison's chamber.

Davison also explored the upper part of the escape shaft, which he called a well. He found it blocked with rubble 200 ft (60 m) down.

"Forty centuries look down on you from these pyramids."

French general Napoleon Bonaparte addressing his troops in Egypt in 1798

More discoveries

In 1798–1801, a French army commanded by Napoleon Bonaparte occupied Egypt. Napoleon had 175 scientists and surveyors with him, and they carried out a survey of Egypt's monuments, including Khufu's pyramid. Later, Italian Giovanni Caviglia discovered the unfinished underground chamber in 1817, and cleared the blocked lower half of the escape shaft, showing that it connected to the descending passage. He also discovered the two mysterious shafts in the King's Chamber.

Entering the pyramids

In 1818, an Italian ex-circus strongman, Giovanni Belzoni, found the upper entrance to Khafra's pyramid. It had been sealed for centuries. Belzoni discovered that it had been robbed, too, and the sarcophagus lid was broken in two pieces. In 1837, Richard Vyse, an English army officer, used gunpowder in Khufu's pyramid to blast a passage above Davison's chamber and found four more chambers. Vyse also used gunpowder on the second and third pyramids. He even drilled a deep, 27-ft (8-m) hole in the back of the Sphinx to find out if it had any inner chambers.

Archaeological digs at Giza could involve dozens of people. This photograph from the 1920s shows the team led by US archaeologist George Reisner.

Scientific study

The first scientific archaeologist to work at Giza was William Flinders Petrie, nicknamed the "father of Egyptian archaeology." In the 1880s, he carried out a detailed survey of the entire Giza plateau, including the Great Pyramid, whose passages and chambers he carefully measured. Petrie was devoted to this task, and even chose to sleep inside a rock tomb so that he could be near the excavation site. Due to the extreme heat, he often wore nothing but his underwear—he noticed that if it was pink he could scare off curious tourists and thus work undisturbed.

Shifting sands have buried the Sphinx many times in its long history, as can be seen in this old photograph. They were most recently cleared away in 1905.

Mark Lehner is one of today's leading Egyptologists. He uses computers to produce incredibly detailed surveys of the whole Giza site.

Rapid progress

During the 20th century, Petrie was followed by many more archaeologists. They included American George Reisner, who discovered the tomb of Khufu's mother, Queen Hetepheres, in 1925. An unrobbed tomb was rare and exciting indeed. This one contained a sealed sarcophagus, which Reisner opened in front of a specially invited audience in March 1927. But to his dismay, it was completely empty. By the 1950s, Egyptian archaeologists were also working at Giza. It was an Egyptian, Kamal el-Mallakh, who discovered Khufu's two intact boat pits in 1954. Since 1990, Egyptian Zahi Hawass and American Mark Lehner have both been working on the Giza plateau. They uncovered the pyramid workers' food-processing area and the cemetery where the workers who built the pyramid were buried.

Weird ideas

Despite everything we have learned, some people refuse to accept the pyramids were built by pharaohs as tombs. Books and websites claim that they were built by aliens or an ancient lost civilization. Zahi Hawass says at his lectures that anyone can make a lot of money from the pyramids—just make up an idea, the crazier the better, and write a book about it! Even today, the pyramids continue to fascinate us.

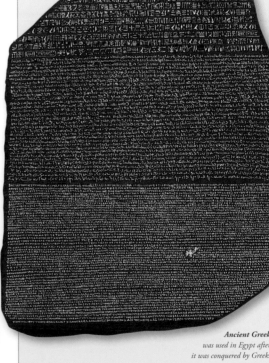

Rosetta Stone

This black basalt slab was found by Napoleon's soldiers at el-Rashid (Rosetta) in 1799. It has writing in Greek, hieroglyphs, and another Egyptian script. By comparing these different translations of the same text, scholars worked out how to read hieroglyphs.

Demotic was an Egyptian script used for handwriting

Hieroglyphs were used in ancient Egypt for religious purposes

Ancient Greek was used in Egypt after it was conquered by Greeks

THE GREAT SPHINX

To the southwest of Khufu's Great Pyramid are two smaller pyramids, built by his son, Khafra, and grandson, Menkaura. Khafra also built a gigantic figure in the desert with the body of a lion and the head of a pharaoh, wearing a royal **nemes** headscarf. This is known as the Sphinx, a Greek name for a mythical creature, part animal and part human. But what did the ancient Egyptians think about this statue? And why did Khafra choose to build it? Visitors to Egypt have argued over these questions for hundreds of years.

The Great Sphinx lies in front of Khafra's own pyramid, which is in the background here. Although this pyramid is smaller than Khufu's, it looks the same size, because Khafra cleverly chose a higher area of land to build on.

The features of the Sphinx match those on life-size statues of Khafra, with broad cheeks and ears that stick out. This suggests that the Sphinx could have been designed to be a self-portrait, glorifying the pharaoh.

The Sphinx lies beside the causeway linking Khafra's pyramid and his valley temple. This is good evidence that it was built for Khafra, not another pharaoh. His workers began by cutting a U-shaped trench to remove sand and rock and expose a mound of bedrock. This was then carved to make the Sphinx.

The Great Sphinx was carved out of limestone **bedrock**. It is just over 236 ft (72 m) long and 65 ft (20 m) high. This was the largest sculpture that Egypt had ever seen, and its size would not be equazled for over a thousand years.

nemes A striped folded headcloth, worn only by a pharaoh.

bedrock The solid rock that lies under soil and surface rock.

THE LEGEND OF TUTHMOSIS

Between the paws of the Sphinx, there is a granite stele, placed there by Pharaoh Tuthmosis IV around 1400 BC. In its inscription, Tuthmosis tells how, as a young prince, he had gone hunting at Giza and fallen asleep in the shadow of the Sphinx. At that time, the Sphinx was partly buried in sand. The Sphinx appeared to him in a dream and promised him the throne of Egypt if he cleared away the sand. Tuthmosis did as he was asked and became king. Pictures on the stele show the grateful pharaoh worshiping the Sphinx.

STELE OF TUTHMOSIS IV

The name Khafra means "appearing like Re," the sun god. During his reign as pharaoh, Khafra also adopted the title *Sa Re*, meaning "Son of Re." The Sphinx faces east toward the rising sun and represents Khafra greeting the life-giving rays of the newborn sun.

Unlike his brother Radjedef, whose pyramid is a few miles north of Giza, Khafra built his pyramid right next to Khufu's Great Pyramid, shown here in the background. Khafra must have admired his father greatly—he chose to spend all eternity at his side.

Lions are often symbols of strength and royalty. Egyptologist Mark Lehner has made a detailed study of the Sphinx. He argues that the combination of a lion's body and the king's head symbolized power controlled by the pharaoh's wisdom.

Over time, the Sphinx has become badly worn and damaged, even losing its nose at some point. It has also been repaired many times, and its sides are now a patchwork of stone blocks added over thousands of years.

Another role of the lion in ancient Egyptian belief was as a guardian of holy places. Khafra possibly built the Sphinx to protect his tomb, the pyramid lying directly behind. Its terrifying grandeur was meant to scare away potential thieves.

stele A carved or inscribed stone slab.

61

CATALOG OF TREASURES

Every single pyramid was looted in ancient times, so we do not know for sure what riches they contained. Luckily, archaeologists have found a few unrobbed tombs near pyramids. Some of the most spectacular finds came from the secret tomb of Khufu's mother, Queen Hetepheres. Buried in an underground chamber next to the Great Pyramid, this had not only exquisite jewelry and fine pottery, but also the oldest known furniture in the world.

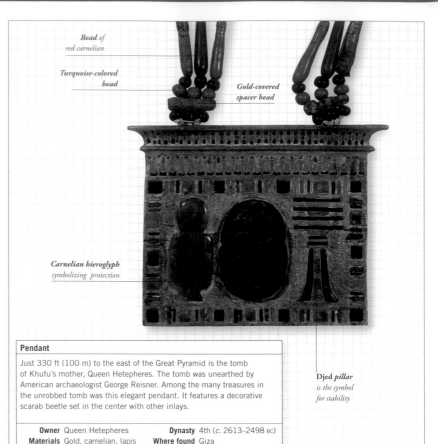

Bead of red carnelian

Turquoise-colored bead

Gold-covered spacer bead

Carnelian hieroglyph symbolizing protection

Djed pillar is the symbol for stability

Pendant

Just 330 ft (100 m) to the east of the Great Pyramid is the tomb of Khufu's mother, Queen Hetepheres. The tomb was unearthed by American archaeologist George Reisner. Among the many treasures in the unrobbed tomb was this elegant pendant. It features a decorative scarab beetle set in the center with other inlays.

Owner Queen Hetepheres	**Dynasty** 4th (*c.* 2613–2498 BC)	
Materials Gold, carnelian, lapis lazuli, turquoise	**Where found** Giza	
	When found 1925	

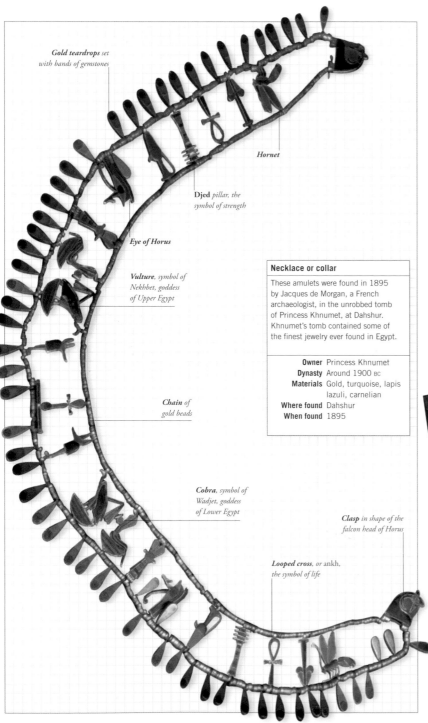

Gold teardrops set with bands of gemstones

Hornet

Djed pillar, the symbol of strength

Eye of Horus

Vulture, symbol of Nekhbet, goddess of Upper Egypt

Chain of gold beads

Cobra, symbol of Wadjet, goddess of Lower Egypt

Clasp in shape of the falcon head of Horus

Looped cross, or ankh, the symbol of life

Necklace or collar

These amulets were found in 1895 by Jacques de Morgan, a French archaeologist, in the unrobbed tomb of Princess Khnumet, at Dahshur. Khnumet's tomb contained some of the finest jewelry ever found in Egypt.

Owner	Princess Khnumet
Dynasty	Around 1900 BC
Materials	Gold, turquoise, lapis lazuli, carnelian
Where found	Dahshur
When found	1895

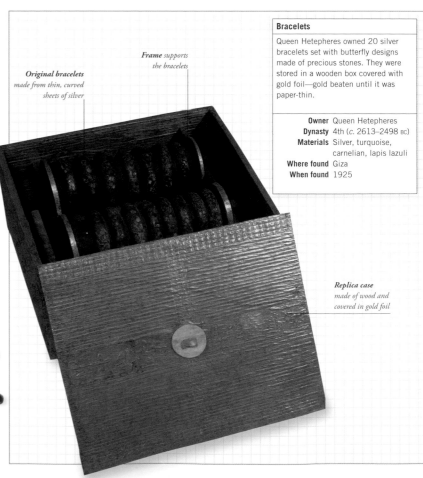

Frame supports the bracelets

Original bracelets made from thin, curved sheets of silver

Replica case made of wood and covered in gold foil

Bracelets

Queen Hetepheres owned 20 silver bracelets set with butterfly designs made of precious stones. They were stored in a wooden box covered with gold foil—gold beaten until it was paper-thin.

Owner	Queen Hetepheres
Dynasty	4th (*c.* 2613–2498 BC)
Materials	Silver, turquoise, carnelian, lapis lazuli
Where found	Giza
When found	1925

Stone vessels

These carved stone pots were found in tombs dating from the time of the earliest pharaohs. Similar pots would have been placed in Khufu's tomb for him to use at mealtimes in the afterlife.

Owner	Not known
Dynasty	1st (*c.* 3100–2890 BC) to 3rd (3100–2613 BC)
Materials	Various types of stone: slate, gneiss, amethyst
Where found	Saqqara

Vase or jug made of slate

Pot carved from amethyst

Bowl made of gneiss

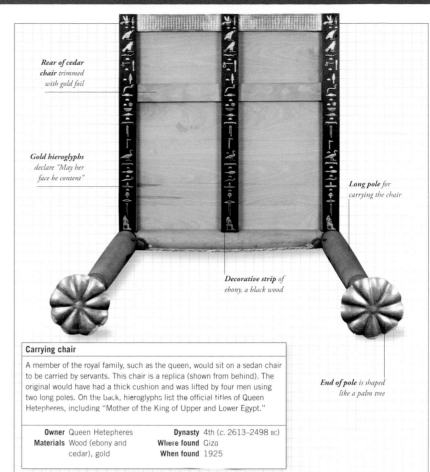

Rear of cedar chair trimmed with gold foil

Gold hieroglyphs declare "May her face be content"

Long pole for carrying the chair

Decorative strip of ebony, a black wood

End of pole is shaped like a palm tree

Carrying chair

A member of the royal family, such as the queen, would sit on a sedan chair to be carried by servants. This chair is a replica (shown from behind). The original would have had a thick cushion and was lifted by four men using two long poles. On the back, hieroglyphs list the official titles of Queen Hetepheres, including "Mother of the King of Upper and Lower Egypt."

Owner	Queen Hetepheres	**Dynasty**	4th (*c.* 2613–2498 BC)
Materials	Wood (ebony and cedar), gold	**Where found**	Giza
		When found	1925

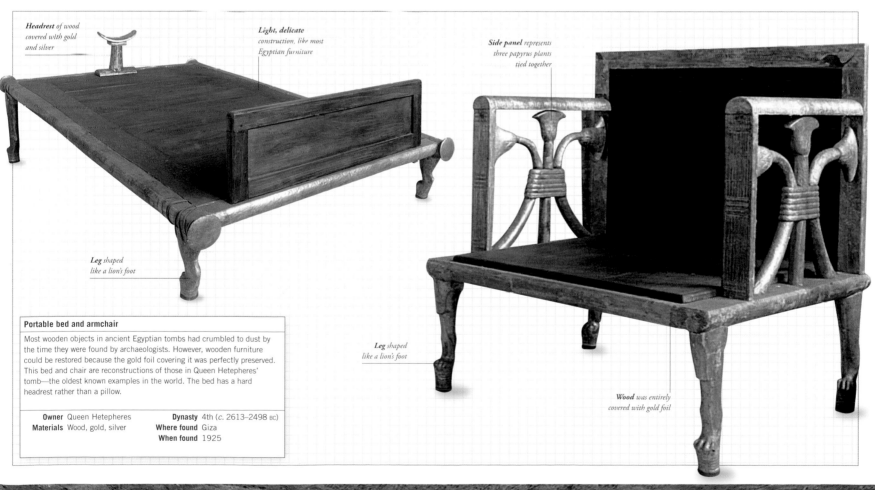

Headrest of wood covered with gold and silver

Light, delicate construction, like most Egyptian furniture

Side panel represents three papyrus plants tied together

Leg shaped like a lion's foot

Leg shaped like a lion's foot

Wood was entirely covered with gold foil

Portable bed and armchair

Most wooden objects in ancient Egyptian tombs had crumbled to dust by the time they were found by archaeologists. However, wooden furniture could be restored because the gold foil covering it was perfectly preserved. This bed and chair are reconstructions of those in Queen Hetepheres' tomb—the oldest known examples in the world. The bed has a hard headrest rather than a pillow.

Owner	Queen Hetepheres	**Dynasty**	4th (*c.* 2613–2498 BC)
Materials	Wood, gold, silver	**Where found**	Giza
		When found	1925

CATALOG OF PYRAMIDS

Kings built pyramids of varying shapes and sizes in ancient Egypt over a period of about 900 years. To understand why Khufu's tomb is called the Great Pyramid, try comparing its plan with those of earlier and later pyramids. Khufu's was not just bigger than all of the others—everything about it was on a more magnificent scale. His pyramid has not only the highest burial chamber, but also the deepest underground chamber—98 ft (30 m) below the ground.

Upper level was built in steps

Burial chamber is underground

Stepped Mastaba (ruined)

A forerunner of the pyramids, this stepped structure was found inside a mastaba at Saqqara. It was a private tomb, not a royal monument. Made of mudbrick, most of it above ground has disappeared.

Pharaoh	Possibly Nebitka, a nobleman, not a king
Period	During the 1st dynasty
Base	74.5 x 35 ft (22.7 x 10.6 m)
Height	7.5 ft (2.3 m)
Volume	17,657 cu ft (500 m³)

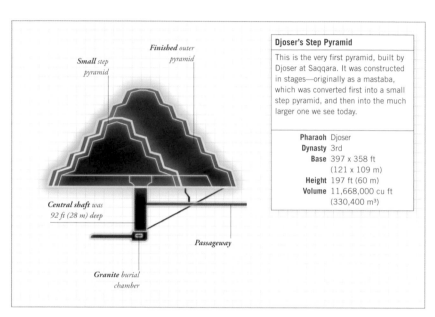

Small step pyramid

Finished outer pyramid

Central shaft was 92 ft (28 m) deep

Passageway

Granite burial chamber

Djoser's Step Pyramid

This is the very first pyramid, built by Djoser at Saqqara. It was constructed in stages—originally as a mastaba, which was converted first into a small step pyramid, and then into the much larger one we see today.

Pharaoh	Djoser
Dynasty	3rd
Base	397 x 358 ft (121 x 109 m)
Height	197 ft (60 m)
Volume	11,668,000 cu ft (330,400 m³)

The pyramid-builders

In around 300 BC, an Egyptian priest called Manetho listed all the known pharaohs, placing them in 31 dynasties. Each dynasty was a series of rulers from the same family. Experts still debate the numbers and dates of the dynasties. Here is a list of rulers at the time of the pyramids.

1st Dynasty	3000–2890 BC	Seven pharaohs, ruling after the unification of Egypt
2nd Dynasty	2890–2686 BC	Between seven and ten pharaohs
3rd Dynasty	2686–2613 BC	Five or six pharaohs, including Djoser
4th Dynasty	2613–2498 BC	Six pharaohs, including Snefru, Khufu, Radjedef, and Khafra
5th Dynasty	2494–2345 BC	Eight or nine pharaohs, including Userkaf and Nyuserra
6th Dynasty	2345–2181 BC	Between four and six pharaohs, including Teti
7th/8th Dynasties	2181–2125 BC	Unknown number of pharaohs, including Ibi
9th/10th Dynasties	2160–2055 BC	Unknown number of pharaohs, who might have built some pyramids
11th Dynasty	2125–1985 BC	Seven pharaohs, who did not build any pyramids
12th Dynasty	1985–1795 BC	Eight pharaohs, including Senusret I
13th Dynasty	1795–1725 BC	Unknown number of pharaohs, including Khendjer

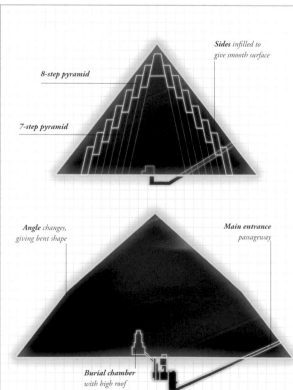

Sides infilled to give smooth surface

8-step pyramid

7-step pyramid

Angle changes, giving bent shape

Main entrance passageway

Burial chamber with high roof

Snefru's First Pyramid

At Meidum, Snefru began by building a pyramid with seven steps, which was then enlarged to eight. Much later, the steps were filled in to make a smooth-sided pyramid, which now lies in ruins.

Pharaoh	Snefru
Dynasty	4th
Base	472 x 472 ft (144 x 144 m)
Height	302 ft (92 m)
Volume	22,557,000 cu ft (638,733 m³)

Snefru's Bent Pyramid

With his second attempt, this time at Dahshur, Snefru's architects made the angle of the pyramid's sides too steep. This meant too much weight was placed on the foundations, and so the angle was reduced halfway up.

Pharaoh	Snefru
Dynasty	4th
Base	617 x 617 ft (188 x 188 m)
Height	345 ft (105 m)
Volume	43,686,000 cu ft (1,237,040 m³)

Smooth sides

Entrance passageway

Burial chamber with high roof

Antechamber

Snefru's North Pyramid

Also known as the Red Pyramid, this was the third pyramid built by Snefru. Located at Dahshur, its sides sloped more gently than the Bent Pyramid nearby. Snefru probably could have built a steeper-sided structure, but he did not want to take any chances after the problems caused by the Bent Pyramid. Like both of his previous pyramids, the burial chamber here had a high, stepped roof.

Pharaoh	Sneferu	**Height** 345 ft (105 m)
Dynasty	4th	**Volume** 59,823,000 cu ft (1,694,000 m³)
Base	722 x 722 ft (220 x 220 m)	

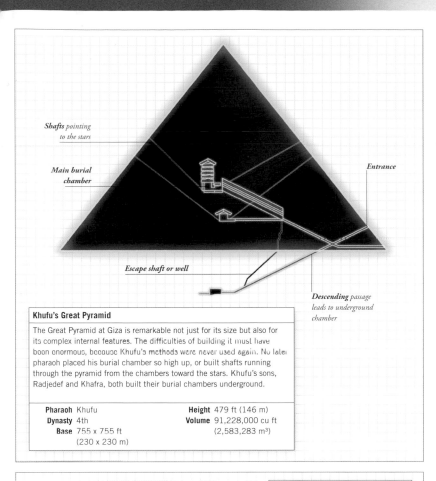

Shafts pointing
to the stars

*Main burial
chamber*

Entrance

Escape shaft or well

Descending passage
leads to underground
chamber

Khufu's Great Pyramid

The Great Pyramid at Giza is remarkable not just for its size but also for its complex internal features. The difficulties of building it must have been enormous, because Khufu's methods were never used again. No later pharaoh placed his burial chamber so high up, or built shafts running through the pyramid from the chambers toward the stars. Khufu's sons, Radjedef and Khafra, both built their burial chambers underground.

Pharaoh	Khufu	**Height**	479 ft (146 m)
Dynasty	4th	**Volume**	91,228,000 cu ft
Base	755 x 755 ft		(2,583,283 m³)
	(230 x 230 m)		

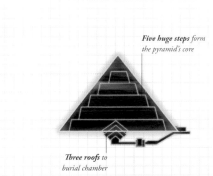

Five huge steps form
the pyramid's core

Three roofs to
burial chamber

Teti's Pyramid

Teti and pharaohs of the sixth dynasty continued the fifth-dynasty custom of building pyramids with stepped cores, and burial chambers with angled beams in the roofs. Teti's burial chamber has three roofs on top of each other.

Pharaoh	Teti
Dynasty	6th
Base	258 x 258 ft
	(78.75 x 78.75 m)
Height	172 ft (52.5 m)
Volume	3,808,000 cu ft
	(107,835 m³)

Pyramids of the world

Pyramids were the world's first massive stone buildings. Since the pharaohs, many peoples around the world have built pyramids. The best known, in Mexico and Central America, were mostly temples rather than tombs. Modern pyramids use a variety of spectacular materials.

Mesoamerican pyramids The largest pyramid in America is Teotihuacan, the Pyramid of the Sun, an ancient temple built in central Mexico between AD 150 and 650. Its base is about the same size as Egypt's Great Pyramid, but it is only half the height. We still do not know who built it, or why.

Mayan pyramids The Maya of Central America existed from about AD 300 to 900. They built pyramids as temples that were often royal tombs as well. This was because they worshiped dead kings as gods. On top of the pyramid was a small temple where the dead king lying beneath was worshiped.

Aztec pyramids The Aztec civilization of Mexico reached its height in about 1400–1520. It built impressive pyramids as temples to Huitzilopochtli, the war god, and Tlaloc, the rain god. On top of the pyramids, prisoners captured in war were sacrificed as offerings to them.

Louvre pyramid Perhaps the most famous modern pyramid is in the courtyard of the Louvre, an art museum in Paris. Made of glass and steel, it is 71 ft (21.6 m) high. It serves as the entrance to the museum's underground galleries, and allows light to flood in. The architect was I. M. Pei.

Userkaf's Pyramid

Pharaoh Userkaf, the founder of the fifth dynasty, roofed his burial chamber in a new way. He used huge limestone beams, placed at a sharp angle against each other. This method protected the burial chamber from the weight above.

Pharaoh	Userkaf
Dynasty	5th
Base	240 x 240 ft
	(73.3 x 73.3 m)
Height	161 ft (49 m)
Volume	3,104,000 cu ft
	(87,906 m³)

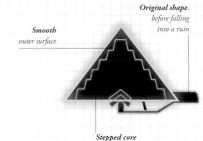

Angled beams support
massive weight above
burial chamber

Original shape,
before falling
into a ruin

Smooth
outer surface

Stepped core

Nyuserra's Pyramid

Userkaf was followed by four pharaohs, including Nyuserra, who built their pyramids at Abusir. They constructed them using stepped cores, which were then filled in to make smooth-sided pyramids.

Pharaoh	Niuserre
Dynasty	5th
Base	259 x 259 ft
	(78.9 m x 78.9)
Height	170 ft (51.7 m)
Volume	3,978,000 cu ft
	(112,632 m³)

Original shape,
before falling
into a ruin

Ibi's Pyramid (ruined)

The only surviving pyramid of the eighth dynasty, this one at Saqqara was later almost completely destroyed by stone thieves. The surviving ruins are just 10 ft (3 m) high, but it may have been seven times higher when completed.

Pharaoh	Ibi
Dynasty	8th
Base	103 x 103 ft
	(31.5 m x 31.5 m)
Height	Possibly 69 ft (21 m)
Volume	Possibly 247,000 cu ft
	(6,994 m³)

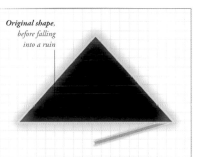

Original shape,
before falling
into a ruin

Senusret I's Pyramid (ruined)

Pyramid-building revived under this pharaoh. At Lisht he built on a scale unmatched since the fifth dynasty. His burial chamber is so deep that it has never been found. Attempts to reach it are blocked by water underground.

Pharaoh	Senusret I
Dynasty	12th
Base	344 x 344 ft
	(105 x 105 m)
Height	201 ft (61.25 m)
Volume	7,949,000 cu ft
	(225,093 m³)

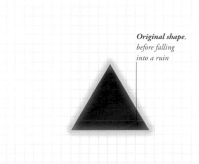

Original shape,
before falling
into a ruin

Khendjer's Pyramid (ruined)

Khendjer was one of the last pharaohs to build a pyramid. Sited at Saqqara, it had a mudbrick core with limestone casing. Mudbrick was an easier material to use, but the finished appearance was the same as a stone monument.

Pharaoh	Khendjer
Dynasty	13th
Base	172 x 172 ft
	(52.5 x 52.5 m)
Height	121 ft (37 m)
Volume	1,557,000 cu ft
	(44,096 m³)

INDEX

A page number in **bold** refers to the main entry for that subject